# Church History

by

## Aude McKee

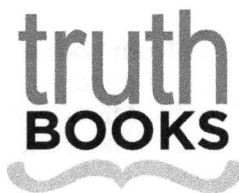

truth
BOOKS

ISBN 10: 1-58427-348-8

ISBN 13: 978-1-58427-348-6

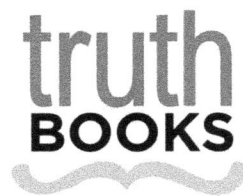

**truth**
**BOOKS**

**Guardian of Truth Foundation**
**C E I Bookstore**
**220 South Marion, Athens, AL 35611**
**www.CEIbooks.com**
**1-855-49-BOOKS or 1-855-492-6657**

# Table of Contents

# Preface

This material was prepared and delivered as sermons at the West Knoxville church of Christ, Knoxville, TN. This accounts for the lack of documentation in a number of places. At this point in time it would be impossible for me to express appreciation to every author but the first two volumes of *The Search for the Ancient Order* by Earl I. West, *History of the Reformation of the Sixteenth Century* by J. H. D'Aubigne, D.D., *A Manual of Church History* by Albert Henry Newman, and *History of the Christian Church* by W. M. Blackburn, D.D. were helpful to me.

## LESSON 1
# Origin of the Lord's Church

**Introduction:**
I.  Definitions.
    A.  Origin: Coming into existence or use; beginning.
    B.  Church
        1.  Greek word for "church" is *ekklesia.*
            a.  Word means "called out."
            b.  People (Acts 8:3).
        2.  To understand what the church is, one must understand the nature of the call.
            a.  By God (Phil. 3:13-14).
            b.  From sin (Eph. 5:22-27).
            c.  By the gospel (2 Thess. 2:14).
            d.  In obedience (Rom. 6:17-18).
II. Not discussing the origin of men's churches – that study will come in later lessons. This lesson is the origin of the Lord's church (Matt. 16:18).

**Discussion:**
**I.  The origin of the Lord's church can be determined by an examination of prophecy.**
    A.  The Saviour promised:
        1.  Seed promise.
            a.  Gen. 3:15.
            b.  Gen. 22:18; 21:12.
            c.  Mal. 3:1-3 (Rom. 9:13).
            d.  Gen. 49:10.
            e.  Psa. 132:11.
        2.  Note Matthew's lineage – Abraham to Christ (Matt. 1).
    B.  Christ's rule over His people is promised.
        1.  The kingdom to be established:
            a.  Dan. 2:44.
            b.  Dan. 7:13-14.
            c.  Matt. 3:1-2.
            d.  Mk. 1:14-15.
            e.  Matt. 16:18-19.
            f.  Mk. 9:1.
            g.  Lk. 24:46-49.
            h.  Acts 1:8.
        2. Climax – Acts 2.

**II. Can be determined by the composition of the church.**
    A.  Note again the meaning of the word "church" – people called out of sin in obedience to the gospel of Christ."
        1.  2 Thess. 2:14.
        2.  Rom. 1:16.
        3.  1 Pet. 1:23.
        4.  Jas. 1:27.
        5.  Mk. 16:15-16.

      6.  2 Tim. 1:8-10.

B.  What is the gospel?
1.  1 Pet. 1:22-23.
2.  Of what composed?
    a.  Facts to be believed (1 Cor. 15:1-4).
    b.  Commands to be obeyed (Rom. 10:16; 2 Thess. 1:7-9; Rom. 6:11-18; 1 Pet. 4:17).
    c.  Promises to be trusted (Mk. 16:15-16; Acts 2:38; 5:32; 2 Pet. 1:10-11).

C.  For the church to be established there had to be:
1.  Facts to be believed.
2.  Commands to obey.
3.  Promises to be trusted.

D.  First time these factors all were present – Day of Pentecost, Acts 2.

**III.  Can be determined by its purchase price.**

A.  Bought by the precious blood of Christ.
1.  Acts 20:28.
2.  Eph. 5:23-27.

B.  What did the blood literally purchase?
1.  1 Pet. 2:5; 1 Tim. 3:15.
2.  1 Pet. 1:18-19.

C.  The blood was shed on the cross after Jesus was dead (Jn. 19:31-37).
1.  Church could not have been established in the days of Abraham, David, or even John the Baptist – no "money" yet with which to purchase it.
2.  Church was not established during personal ministry of Christ – blood not yet shed.
3.  On the Day of Pentecost, people were told how to reach the blood. The church had its origin.

**Conclusion:**
1.  All three lines of argument have their apex on the day of Pentecost.
2.  This is the birthday of the Lord's church.
3.  Serious question for you – have you obeyed the gospel? Have you had your sins washed away in His blood?
4.  These questions are the same as asking, are you a member of the Lord's church?

# Questions

**Fill in the Blanks**

1.  The Greek word for "church" means _____ .
2.  _____ is the one who does the calling.
3.  The _____ is God's calling power.
4.  The gospel can be understood and obeyed only by _____ .
5.  In Romans 6:17-18, freedom from sin comes at the point of _____ .

**Short Answer**

1.  To whom did the Old Testament seed promise refer? _____
2.  In the conflict between the Seed and Satan, what was each one to receive?

    _____

3.  When was the seed promise fulfilled and who was to be blessed? _____

    _____

4.  During the reign of what empire was the Lord's kingdom established? _____

    _____

5.  According to Daniel, when was the kingdom to be given to the Son of man?

    _____

6. According to Mark, the kingdom was to come in what time frame? _____
   _____

7. On what occasion did the Lord's authority begin to be proclaimed world-
   wide?_____
   _____

8. When did people first obey the gospel? _____

9. A body is composed of members and a temple of stones. Of what is a kingdom
   composed? _____
   _____

10. What was the purchase price of the Lord's church? _____
    _____

**Projects**

1. Make a list of all the things in which a kingdom and the church are alike. ____
   _____
   _____

2. Make a list of the figures used by the Holy Spirit to describe the church._____
   _____
   _____

3. Prepare a list of the reasons why the church could not have been established
   by John the Baptist or in his lifetime. _____
   _____
   _____

4. List the passages in the book of Acts where the word "Kingdom" is used. ____
   _____
   _____

5. List those passages in Acts where the word "church" is found. _____
   _____
   _____

## Lesson 2
# The Church: Growth and Apostasy

**Introduction:**
I.   Review of the origin of the Lord's church.
   A.   Through the "seed" all nations were to be blessed. The church is that which the "seed" accomplished (Gen. 3:15; 22:18; Acts 2:47).
   B.   The kingdom was prophesied – Jesus' reign began on Pentecost.
   C.   The church is composed of called out people. This calling is done by the gospel (2 Thess. 2:14) and man responds to the gospel by obeying it (Rom. 6:17-18). The gospel was first preached and people first obeyed on Pentecost day, in Jerusalem, as recorded in Acts 2.
   D.   The church was purchased by the blood of Christ. That blood was shed on the cross, after Jesus died, and the obedience necessary to contact that blood was first made known on Pentecost day (Acts 20:28; 1 Pet. 1:18-19; Jn. 19:31-37; Acts 2:37-38).
II.  In this lesson we notice the growth of that divine body and then the apostasy that came in later years.

**Discussion:**
I.   **The book of Acts beginning at chapter 2 is a history of the church – divine church history.**
   A.   From a small beginning it grew to be a mighty force in the world (Matt. 13:31-32).
      1.   3000 added the first day (Acts 2:41).
      2.   Soon the number of men was about 5000.
      3.   Multitudes both of men and women were added to the Lord (Acts 5:14).
      4.   In those days the number of disciples was multiplied (Acts 6:1).
      5.   Within 30 years Paul could say that the gospel had come to all the world and that every creature under heaven had been preached to (Col. 1:5-6, 23).
   B.   The book of Acts is a record of the work of Peter, Philip, Stephen, Paul, Silas, Barnabas, and others. But the rapid growth of the church could not have been accomplished by the work of these men alone. All the members of the church were proclaimers of the Word – the seed of the kingdom (Acts 8:4). They planted and watered; God gave the increase (1 Cor. 3:6).
   C.   The book of Acts records the beginning of the church in many different cities: Jerusalem, Acts 2; Samaria, 8:5-12; Caesarea, 10; Antioch of Syria, 11:19-21; Paphos and Antioch of Pisidia, 13:6-49; Iconium and Lystra, 14:1-23; Philippi, 16:12-40; Thessalonica, Berea, Athens, 17:1-34; Corinth, 18:1-11.

II.  **The seed that produces the church is that which determines every characteristic of it.**
   A.   The seed (Word of God, the gospel) saves (makes people members of the called-out).
      1.   2 Thess. 2:14; Rom. 1:16; Jas.1:21; 1 Pet. 1:23.
      2.   That Word has to be respected deeply enough to render obedience (1 Pet. 1:22; Rom. 6:17-18).

B. Continued respect and obedience must characterize the church.
  1. Jude 3; 2 Tim. 3:16-17; Gal. 1:8-9; 2 Jn. 9.
  2. The church is the one body; that one body is ruled by one head (Eph. 4:4; Col. 1:18; Matt. 28:18; Eph. 5:23-24).
C. Respect for divine authority will produce many distinctive and identifying features of the Lord's church. Among them:
  1. Doctrine or teaching, name, worship, work, organization, purity of life.
  2. A lack of respect for divine authority will produce corruptions in doctrine, name, worship, work, organization, and purity of life.

III. **The departures from God's order and way should have come as no surprise. Christians had been warned!**
  A. Paul's inspired predictions:
    1. Acts 20:28-32.
    2. 1 Tim. 4:1-5.
    3. 2 Tim. 4:1-4.
    4. 2 Thess. 2:1-12.
  B. They could have looked about them for evidence that man is prone to depart.
    1. In history:
      a. Adam and Eve were not satisfied with God's perfect order of things.
      b. Adam's descendants departed so far that God found the flood necessary.
      c. The history of the Jewish people is a history of their departures from God's law.
    2. Early in the church's history there were departures from the divine order.
      a. False teaching concerning circumcision and keeping the law (Acts 15; book of Galatians; Col. 2; Heb. 7, 8, 9).
      b. Bad conditions existed in the Corinthian church.
        (1) Sectarianism – too high regard for men (1 Cor. 1-3)
        (2) Fornication (1 Cor. 5).
        (3) Going to law with brethren (1 Cor. 6).
        (4) Corruption of the Lord's supper (1 Cor. 11).
        (5) Denying the resurrection (1 Cor. 15).
      c. There were those who were set on "one-man-rule" (3 Jn. 9-10).
      d. Five of the seven Asian churches were not faultless.
        (1) Ephesus had left her first love (Rev. 2:4).
        (2) Some at Pergamos held to the doctrine of Balaam and the Nicolaitanes (2:14-15).
        (3) The church in Thyatira allowed Jezebel to seduce the Lord's servants (2:20).
        (4) The church in Sardis was dead (3:1).
        (5) Laodicea was lukewarm (3:16).
    3. As the years went on, many false teachings and practices were brought in.
      a. Penance, 157 A.D.; First church council – first creed, 325; Mass introduced, 394; Image worship, 405; Extreme unction, 588; Purgatory, 593; Instrumental music, 670; Celibacy, 1015.
    4. The most significant of these departures is that of 325 A.D. It symbolized the removing of the authority from Jesus, the head, and placing it in the hands of men. With this step taken, the hope of turning back was small indeed.
      a. About the year 318 a controversy arose in Alexandria respecting the person of Christ: was He eternal and divine just as God the Father, or was He a creature, created by God?
      b. Constantine, the Roman Emperor, though not a Christian, was kindly disposed toward the teachings of Christ. He was anxious

**Notes**

to have peace and so he called a council of church leaders to be held in Nicea in June, 325. A great number attended and during this meeting the decision was reached that Christ was eternal with the Father. This decision was then written and carried back to the churches and they were expected to accept it.

    c. The power to decide truth, then, was removed from Christ and His Word and placed in the hands of delegates from churches! It takes no Solomon to see that the step from this to placing the determination of truth in the hands of one man (the Pope) is not too great!

**Conclusion:**
1. Apostasy is rooted in a lack of respect for divine authority.
2. The truth of God will produce the church; only the truth of God, faithfully followed, will assure God's approval here and His welcome words, "Enter thou into the joys of thy Lord."
3. Every individual who is past the age of accountability has experienced apostasy in his own life.
   a. Born free of sin, pure, and holy.
   b. Apostasy came when God's will was not followed.
   c. The way back is just the reverse of Apostasy's course.

# Questions

**Truth or False**

_____ 1. "Slow and steady" would describe the growth of the church in the first century.

_____ 2. Peter said that the gospel had been preached to every creature under heaven.

_____ 3. The Christians who were scattered, went everywhere seeking employment.

_____ 4. Respect for divine authority is essential to being a Christian and to continued faithfulness.

_____ 5. The church was free of problems in the first century.

**Supply the Missing Word**
1. The head of the church. _____
2. Those who demanded Gentiles be circumcised. _____
3. The man who loved pre-eminence. _____
4. The church that was lukewarm. _____
5. The date for the introduction of instrumental music to the worship. _____

**Short Answer**
1. Does the church have a proper name like "John Doe"? _____
2. Do you think it is possible to have a denominational concept of the Lord's church? _____
3. If your answer to the above is "yes," list some ways this concept may be recognized. _____
4. What, would you say, is the only fool-proof guarantee against apostasy?
5. What does "remove the candlestick" (Rev. 2:5) imply?_____
6. According to Paul, apostasy would come from among what group of men?

       *Church History*

7.  List the characteristics of apostasy from 1 Timothy 4 and 2 Timothy. _____

    _____

    _____

    _____

8.  About when was the church in Ephesus established? _____

    About what date was Revelation 2:1-7 written? _____

9.  Can a disputed doctrinal point be decided by a gathering of the "best minds" among us? _____

10. What passage shows that the attitude that brings apostasy existed in the first century? _____

## Lesson 3
# The Rise of Catholicism

**Introduction:**

I.   Review of past lessons.

A.   We have studied the origin of the Lord's church. It had its beginning on the day of Pentecost, in Jerusalem, in the 33rd year following the birth of Christ. The record of that beginning is found in Acts 2.

B.   In the last lesson we observed two things: the growth of the church and the beginning of apostasy.

1.   The church, from a humble beginning, grew to be a mighty army of saints.

2.   But even during this period of growth, warnings were sounded by the Spirit.

3.   Lack of respect for divine authority brought departures from God's pattern.

II.  We are now prepared to proceed and observe the rise of the world's first denomination. As we trace the origin of Catholicism, we will be simply tracing departures from God's Law.

**Discussion:**

I.   **To understand how Catholicism came into existence, it is necessary to have knowledge of the organization of the Lord's church.**

A.   Christ the Head (Col. 1:18; Eph. 1:20-23).

1.   Christ is the head of the church universal.

2.   This is the only organization the church universal has!

B.   Elders to oversee the local church. They watch for souls, rule and feed the flock.

1.   Acts 11:27-30; 14:23; 20:28; Tit. 1:5; 1 Pet. 5:1-4; Heb. 13:17.

2.   There are three Greek words in the New Testament that refer to this office or work:

a.   *Episkopos* translated "bishop" and "overseer."

(1)  Tit. 1:7 (see Tit. 1:5) – "bishop."

(2)  Phil. 1:1 – "bishop."

(3)  Acts 20:28 – "overseers."

b.   *Poimen* translated "pastor" and "shepherd."

(1)  Eph. 4:11 – "pastors."

(2)  1 Pet. 2:25; 5:1 – "shepherd."

c.   *Presbuteros* translated "presbyter" and "elder."

(1)  Acts 14:23; 1 Tim. 5:17 – "elders."

(2)  1 Tim. 4:14 – "presbytery."

3.   In each local church there was a plurality (more than one) of elders (Acts 14:23; 20:17; Phil. 1:1; Tit. 1:5).

4.   The elders in each local church were *equal* in authority (see every passage where the elders are mentioned).

5.   The elders had authority (rule, oversight, responsibility) *only* in the local church that appointed them.

a.   Acts 20:28; I Pet. 5:1-3.

b.   Their authority (rule, oversight, responsibility) did *not* extend beyond the "flock of God among them."

C. Deacons to serve.
   1. See Phil. 1:1; Acts 6:1-7; 1 Tim. 3:8-13.
   2. Deacons are not overseers – they are special servants.
D. Evangelists, teachers, and saints (Eph. 4:11; Phil. 1:1).

II. **Early in the church's history, elders began to extend their authority.**
  A. Step 1 – distinction made between bishop and elder (see Tit. 1:5, 7).
    1. Natural in group of three or four or more men for one to be outstanding in ability and leadership (and occasionally in ambition to usurp authority).
    2. Gradually, as men's respect for Bible authority lessened, the church drifted into the practice of giving more authority to one man among the elders. This man they designated the "president" or the "presiding bishop."
    3. Thus the word *bishop* came at length to be applied exclusively to one elder and the rest were designated "elders" or "presbyters."
    4. This is an example of a scriptural words being used unscripturally.
  B. Step 2 – extension of the authority of the bishop to congregations other than the one that appointed him.
    1. The city church would establish churches in the neighboring towns and villages. Instead of recognizing the new congregations as independent bodies of Christians, the city church would control them through the bishop.
    2. Gradually, as the city Bishops extended their authority, they became known as Metropolitan Bishops.
  C. Step 3 – the combining of churches of a large area under a single government.
    1. The area became known as a *diocese*.
    2. One of the Metropolitan Bishops graduated into a Diocesan Bishop.
  D. Step 4 – by the close of the 5th century, the octopus of ecclesiasticism had spread until five centers ruled "christendom."
    1. Five Bishops became known as *Patriarchs*.
    2. The centers from which they ruled were Alexandria, Jerusalem, Antioch, Constantinople, and Rome.
  E. Step 5 – the development of the Pope.
    1. In 588, John the Faster, Patriarch of Constantinople, declared himself Universal Bishop.

> "In the year 588, John, Bishop of Constantinople, surnamed the Faster, on account of his extraordinary abstinence and austerity, assembled, by his own authority a council at Constantinople to inquire into an accusation brought against Peter, Patriarch of Antioch; and upon this occasion assumed the title of ecumenical or universal bishop" (Mosheim, *Ecclesiastical History*, Vol. 1, 145).

    2. Gregory the Great, then Patriarch of Rome, declared such an assumption as apostasy, and the one guilty of it "anti-Christ." So in 588, the Catholic Church did not yet exist in its present-day governmental form.

> "... Gregory I was provoked and irritated beyond measure by the assumption of his Eastern rival, and strained every nerve to procure a revocation of that title. He characterized it as a foolish, proud, profane, wicked, pestiferous, blasphemous, and diabolical usurpation, and compared him who used it to Lucifer.... After the death of John the Faster in 596, Gregory instructed his ambassador at Constantinople to demand from the new Patriarch, Cyriacus, as a condition of inter-communion, the renunciation of the wicked title, and in a letter to Maurice, he went so far as to declare, that 'Whosoever calls himself universal priest

or desires to be called so, was the forerunner of Anti-Christ'" (Schaff, *History of the Christian Church*, Vol. III, p. 220).

3. In 606, Boniface III, who had become Patriarch of Rome, acquired for himself the title of Universal Bishop.

> "The disputes about pre-eminence, that had so long subsisted between the bishops of Rome and Constantinople, proceeded, in this century (7th) to such violent lengths, as laid the foundation of that deplorable schism, which afterwards separated the Greek and Latin churches....Boniface III engaged (the emperor) Phocas, that abominable tyrant ... to take from the bishop of Constantinople the title of ecumenical or universal bishop, and to confer it upon the Roman pontiff ... thus was the papal supremacy first introduced" (Mosheim, *Ecclesiastical History*, 1, p. 160).

**III. The Catholic Church was born in the vacuum formed by the fall of the Roman Empire.**
  A. The Roman Empire existed from 27 B.C. to 476 A.D. (some list the fall as 395 A.D.).
    1. Rome had ruled the world and then fell because of internal corruption.
    2. Rome had ruled through a pyramid form of government.
    3. This formed a perfect situation for the creation of the Pope.
  B. 2 Thess. 2:1-12.
    1. The "man of sin" could well be the Catholic Church.
    2. V. 7 points out that something restrained the "man of sin" from making his appearance, but that the restraining force would be removed. This could very well refer to the old Roman Empire.

**IV. The formation of the Catholic Church was not revolutionary, but evolutionary.**
  A. As a flower develops from the seed to the plant to the bud to the blossom, so the Catholic Church developed over a period of 500 years.
    1. In fact, the Catholic Church is still developing – it is a continually developing religious and political organization.
    2. Every few years, new and unscriptural doctrines are adopted and enforced.
  B. The seed from which the Catholic Church sprang was a lack of respect for God and His Son, and an improper attitude toward the Word.
    1. Departures from truth usually do not occur in one mighty leap, but they come gradually. Usually the common folk are able to swallow only a small dose of deviation from truth at a time.
    2. But step after step after step away from God's Word will eventually result in complete apostasy. Thus the Catholic Church is an apostate body.
    3. 1 Jn. 1:6-7; 2 Jn. 9-11.

**Conclusion:**
  1. At this point in our study, religious confusion seems uncalled for.
  2. If you had been living in 610 A.D., and wanted to go to heaven, would you have joined the Catholic Church or would you have simply obeyed the teachings of the gospel and been a Christian, a member of the church Jesus built?
  3. Our plea today is, do nothing, obey nothing, be nothing but that which the New Testament teaches!
  4. By obeying from the heart the simple teachings of Christ (Rom. 6:17-18), salvation must come – the right relationship with the Lord and the Lord's people must necessarily follow!

**Matching**

_____ 1. Deacon        A. Preacher
_____ 2. Elder         B. Formation of Catholicism
_____ 3. Evangelist    C. Special servant
_____ 4. Evolutionary  D. Pyramid
_____ 5. Roman government  E. Overseer

**Short Answer**

1. What is the fundamental idea in each of these words:
   a. Elder? _____
   b. Bishop?_____
   c. Pastor? _____
2. Where are the qualifications for elder found? _____
   _____
3. How do the qualifications for deacon differ from those of an elder?_____
   _____
   _____
4. What limit did the Lord place on the authority of elders? _____
   _____
5. Describe in your own words how the Catholic Church came into existence.
   _____
   _____
   _____
6. Does apostasy take place in one giant leap? _____ If your answer is "no,"
   explain. _____
   _____
7. About how many years did it take for the headship of religious people to be
   transferred from heaven to Rome?_____
8. About how many years passed from the fall of Rome to the first pope?_____
9. Can you find a passage in the Bible that places Peter in Rome at any time for
   any reason? _____
10. List the reasons you can think of that would prohibit Peter from being a pope.
   _____
   _____
   _____

**Underline**

1. The word "pastor" identifies the (preacher, elder, deacon).
2. The word "saint" describes a (set apart, sinless, dead) person.
3. If you had been living in 700 A.D., you could have had your choice (one, many, few) denominations to join.
4. A bishop is a person who is (over, under, the same as) an elder.
5. Most of today's lesson is dependent on (divine, secular) history.

# Lesson 4
# Catholic Dogmas (1)

**Note:** Every quotation from Catholic writers is made from a book bearing the imprimatur of the Roman Catholic Church.

**Introduction:**

I. Thus far in our study we have traced the origin and early growth of the Lord's church. We have also given attention to the warnings about apostasy sounded by the Holy Spirit.

II. In the last lesson we traced the rise of the Catholic system.

   A. Departures came in teaching, worship, work, and religious practices.

   B. The rise of Catholicism can most vividly be traced in the departures from God's pattern in organization.

      1. Organization of the New Testament church.

         a. Christ – head of the church universal.

         b. Each local congregation overseen by elders (bishops).

      2. Three fundamental points were made regarding elders:

         a. Each local church had a plurality.

         b. Elders in each local church were equal in authority.

         c. The elders had authority only in and over the local church that appointed them.

      3. These fundamental principles were ignored. Elders extended their authority until finally in 606 A.D., Boniface III, Patriarch of Rome, declared himself the Universal Bishop. It took hundreds of years for the church to go into apostasy, but eventually the process was completed.

III. In this lesson we study some of the basic things that make Catholicism what it is.

**Discussion:**

**I. Attitude Toward the Bible.**

   A. *The Catholic Church makes the claim that the Bible is a Catholic Book.*

      1. Following are quotations from an advertisement placed in the newspaper by the Supreme Council of Knights of Columbus Religious Information Bureau, St. Louis, MO:

         a. "Yes, the Bible is truly a Catholic book. They were members of the Catholic Church who, under God's inspiration, wrote the New Testament in its entirety."

         b. "It was the Catholic Church which treasured it and gave it to the world in its original and unaltered form."

      2. In the light of this claim, the following questions need to be answered: If the Bible is a Catholic book, then....

         a. Why is it not accepted as their authority in religion?

         b. Why does the name "Catholic" or "Catholic Church" not appear therein?

         c. Why is there no mention made in the Bible of the "Pope," or of his exalted position in the church?

         d. Why is there no reference to Peter as the Vicar of Christ on earth or of his being the head of the church?

e. Why does the Bible say that Peter was a married man (1 Cor. 9:5)?

f. Why is praying to Mary not mentioned in the Bible?

g. Why is the Bible so silent about the doctrines of "Purgatory," "Limbo," "The Rosary," "The Mass," "Auricular Confession," or "Indulgences"?

h. Why does the Bible expressly forbid the making or bowing down to images (Exod. 20:4-5), and the calling of a "priest" by the name of "Father" (Matt. 23:5-12)?

3. The fact of the matter is, the Bible was written between 1500 B.C. and 96 A.D., hundreds of years before the Catholic church was born. The Catholic Church is too young to be the mother of the Bible – a mother must be older than her offspring! The Bible is not a Catholic book!

B. *The Scriptures are not inspired and are not infallible.*

1. "Is the Bible the Infallible Word of God?...The Catholic's answer is a decisive 'No!' Indeed, it is only by the divine authority of the Catholic Church that Christians know that the Scripture is the Word of God and what books certainly belong to the Bible. The Bible is not its own witness. It is like a will without a signature or probate. It is infallible only because of and to the extent of the Church's infallible witness. Deny the Church's infallible witness, and the Bible is at once reduced to the level of mere Oriental literature and utterly devoid of divine inspiration. The Catholic Church alone guarantees infallibly the authenticity of the Latin Vulgate, the contents of the Canon, and the inspiration of all the 72 books of the Holy Writ. As St. Augustine could rightly say in the 5th century, 'I would not believe the Gospel unless moved thereto by the authority of the Church.' The Bible, therefore, is the infallible Word of God only inasmuch as the interpretation of the infallible Church makes it so" (*The Catholic's Question Box* [Herbst], p. 653).

2. See 1 Cor. 2:1-13; Eph. 3:1-7; 1 Thess. 2:13.

C. *The Scriptures are not sufficient.*

1. "The New Testament does not bear the marks of having been drawn up to serve as a code of Christian belief. Neither does it anywhere direct us to take Scripture as our sole Rule of Faith, or free us from the obligation of believing more than is clearly taught in its pages. Therefore, to assume that the Bible is the sole and adequate rule of Christian Faith may perhaps be the only alternative left after rejecting the authority of the Catholic Church; but neither Scripture nor history seems to afford any warrant for such an assumption" (E.R. Hull, *What the Catholic Church Is and What She Teaches*, p. 2).

2. See 2 Tim. 3:16-17; 2 Pet. 1:3.

D. *Traditions are authority.*

1. "The unwritten traditions which we receive from the mouth of Christ himself by the apostles or from the apostles themselves, have come down to us as if delivered from hand to hand on an equality with the books of the Old and New Testaments" (Council of Trent, 16th century).

2. "It would be well to remember that the Bible was never intended to take the place of the living, infallible teacher, the Church, but was written to explain or insist upon a teaching, already preached....The Catholic Church a divine, living, infallible voice, guarantees to every one not merely the written word, but also the unwritten teaching of divine tradition" (*The Catholic's Question Box*, pp. 653-654).

3. See 1 Cor. 4:5; Jn. 20:30-31; Eph. 3:3-4; Rev. 22:18-19; Deut. 4:1-2; 2 Jn. 9-11; Jude 3.

E. *The Common Man is unable to interpret the Scriptures.*

1. "That in matters of faith and morals, and whatever relates to the maintenance of Christian doctrine, no one confiding in his own judgment

shall dare to wrest the sacred Scriptures contrary to that which has been held and still is held by the Holy Mother Church, whose right it is to judge of the true meaning and interpretation of the sacred writ; or contrary to the unanimous consent of the fathers; even though such interpretations should never be published" (Council of Trent, 16th century).

2. See Luke 10:21; Isa. 35:8; 2 Tim. 2:15; 1 Pet. 4:11.

## II. Papal Infallibility.

A. "We the sacred council approving, teach and define that it is a dogma divinely revealed; that the Roman Pontiff, when speaking *ex cathedra*, that is, when discharging the office of pastor and teacher of all Christians, by virtue of his supreme authority, he defines a doctrine regarding faith and morals to be held by the universal church, he by the divine assistance promised to him in the Blessed Peter, is possessed of that infallibility with which the divine Redeemer willed the church should be endowed in defining doctrine regarding faith and morals; and that, therefore such definitions of the Roman Pontiff are irreformable of themselves, and not from the consent of the church. But if any one – which may God avert – presume to contradict our definition, let him be anathema" (*Declaration of Papal Infallibility* made by Pope Pius IX, and adopted by the Vatican Council of 1870).

B. There have been numerous contradictions between popes.
   1. In 1088, Pope Paschall II (and in 1145 Pope Eugenius III) authorized duelling. In 1509, Julius II (and in 1560, Pius IV) forbade it.
   2. In 867, Pope Hadrian declared civil marriages to be valid. In 1800, Pius VII condemned them.
   3. In 1585, Pope Sixtus V published an edition of the Bible and by a bull recommended it to be read. Pius VII condemned the reading of it.
   4. In 1520, Pope Urban VIII excommunicated the famous Italian Galileo and put him in jail because he taught that the earth was round and revolves around the sun. Popes today state that Urban was wrong in condemning the teachings of Galileo.

C. For about 40 years in the 14th century, three men claimed the papacy.

D. Prior to 1870, Catholics denied Papal Infallibility. After 1870, they had to believe it or be guilty of heresy.

E. There have been many wicked popes. Archbishop Purcell, who debated Alexander Campbell, said, "Without doubt some popes are in hell."

## III. Primacy of Peter.

A. "Sitting in that chair in which Peter, the Prince of the Apostles, sat to the close of life, the Catholic Church recognizes in his person the most exalted degree of dignity, and the full jurisdiction not based on constitutions, but emanating from no less authority than from God Himself. As the Successor of St. Peter and the true and legitimate Vicar of Jesus Christ, he therefore, presides over the Universal Church, the Father and Governor of all the faithful, of Bishops, also, and of all other prelates, be their station, rank, or power, what they may be" (Council of Trent, 16th Cent.).

B. Catholic position can be summed up in three points:
   1. Peter was appointed by Christ to be His chief representative and successor and head of the church.
   2. Peter went to Rome and established the "diocese."
   3. Peter's successors (popes) succeeded to his authority.

C. Papal claim based in part on Matthew 16:18-19.
   1. "Thou art Peter (*petros*) and upon this rock (*petra*) I will build my church."
      a. *Petros* is masculine gender – Peter's name.
      b. *Petra* is feminine gender and means "a rock, ledge, cliff."
   2. Jesus had just asked, "Whom do men say I . . . am?" Then He asked, "Whom do you say I am?" Peter replied, "Thou art the Christ, the Son

of the living God." Then the Lord said, "Upon this rock, I will build my church."

. The church was built on Jesus Christ.
   a. Isa. 28:16.
   b. Eph. 2:20; 1 Cor. 3:11.
D. There is no such office as "pope" in the New Testament (1 Cor. 12:28-31; Eph. 4:11-12).
E. Peter never claimed or assumed authority and superiority (Lk. 22:24-27; Gal. 2:11; Acts 10:25-26; 1 Pet. 5:1).
   1. All the apostles were given the same authority Peter had (Matt. 18:18).
   2. Ability to remit and retain sins (by being allowed to reveal the gospel terms of pardon) was given to all the apostles (Jn. 20:23).
   3. Paul was not behind the chiefest apostles (2 Cor. 11:5; 12:11).
F. Peter was a married man (Matt. 8:14; 1 Cor. 9:5).
G. It cannot be proved that Peter was ever in the city of Rome.
   1. Paul wrote the letter to the Roman Christians. In it he saluted 27 people but not Peter. In the Roman letter he did not mention the pope.
   2. Paul wrote four books from Rome but never mentioned Peter or the papacy.
   3. Peter wrote two books of the New Testament. He did not mention Rome or the pope.
   4. No other writer of the New Testament ever mentions Peter and Rome together.

**Conclusion:**
1. As we close this lesson, we need to be reminded of these basic principles:
   a. Jn. 8:32.
   b. Jn. 17:17.
   c. 2 Jn. 9-11.
   d. Jn. 12:48.
2. There is no commodity more precious than truth. May we search for it, believe it, and obey it.

## Questions

**Supply the Missing Word**
1. Area in which the rise of Catholicism can be most easily traced. _____
2. The book that is not of Catholic origin. _____
3. Kind of man who is unable to interpret the Scriptures, according to Catholics.

   _____
4. Obvious fact that disqualifies Peter from being a Pope. _____
5. Number of books that Paul wrote from Rome. _____

**Matching**
_____ 1. Plurality          A. Things handed down
_____ 2. Matthew 23:9       B. An elder
_____ 3. Traditions         C. Elders
_____ 4. Peter              D. Rock
_____ 5. Matthew 16:18      E. Call no man father

**Short Answer**
1. Make one argument showing the Bible is not a Catholic book. _____

2. Is there a single doctrine or practice, that is peculiar to the Catholic Church, that is found in the Bible? _____
3. Define (from your dictionary):
   a. Purgatory: _____

*Catholic Dogmas (1)*                                                    19

    b.  Indulgence: _____

    c.  Rosary: _____

4.  What is unusual about Catholic teaching concerning the Lord's Supper? ___

    _____

5.  To whom do Catholic people confess their sins? _____

    _____

6.  About what date was the writing of the New Testament completed? _____

7.  Does the Catholic Church believe that the Bible is a sufficient guide (see 2 Tim. 3:16-17)?_____

8.  What is meant by "papal infallibility"? _____

    _____

9.  According to Isaiah 28:16, 1 Peter 2:1-8, Acts 4:11-12, Ephesians 2:20, and 1 Corinthians 3:11, upon what is the church built?_____

10. What will make a person free according to John 8:32? _____

    _____

# Lesson 5
# Catholic Dogmas (2)

**Introduction:**

I. History abundantly shows that any time men lose respect for the absolute and complete authority of God's Word, there is no stopping place. As the Holy Spirit stated in 2 Timothy 3:13, "Evil men and seducers shall wax worse and worse, *deceiving and being deceived.*"

  A. As men first began their "progress" away from divine authority, their steps were "small."

  B. Eventually, enough of these steps were put together to carry the church from Jerusalem to Rome – from the church Jesus built to Catholicism!

II. In our last lesson we gave our attention entirely to Catholicism's attitude toward authority. We noted these points:

  A. Catholics claim the Bible is a Catholic Book.

  B. The Scriptures are not inspired and are not infallible.

  C. The Scriptures are not sufficient as a rule of faith and practice.

  D. Traditions are an authority equal with the Old and New Testaments.

  E. The common man is unable to interpret the Scriptures.

  F. The Pope is infallible when speaking *ex cathedra.*

  G. Peter was given primacy – he was the first pope.

III. In this lesson, we notice some of the beliefs and practices of Catholicism that are out-growths of their attitude toward authority.

**Discussion:**

I. **Celibacy (Unmarried Church Officials).**

  A. *The doctrine began in the 4th century.* Celibacy was first enjoined at Rome by Gregory VII in 1073.

  B. *The Council of Trent made the doctrine official church doctrine* with the following proclamation:

  > "If anyone saith that the marriage state is to be preferred before the state of virginity, or celibacy, and that it is not better and more blessed to remain in virginity, or in celibacy, than to be united in matrimony, let him be anathema" (Tenth Canon, Council of Trent). The same Council decreed: "Whoever shall say that the clergy constituted in sacred order, or regulars, who have solemnly professed chastity, may contract marriages and that the contract is valid, let him be accursed."

  C. *In the past, the Church of Rome had imposed universal celibacy on all the "clergy" from Pope to Priest, and from the lowest deacon to the highest Bishop.*

  1. In Vatican II, pressure was brought by liberal bishops for relaxation of the celibate standards.

  2. The law was relaxed only slightly and that for deacons. Men "of more mature age," already married, were allowed to continue in the married state, but for younger men, the law of celibacy remained intact.

  3. The Catholic Church's attitude toward sex and women was expressed by Pope Paul when, in addressing the 13th Congress of the Italian

Women's Center in 1966, he said: "Conjugal chastity...throughout the centuries has redeemed woman from the slavery of a duty submitted to through force and humiliation."

  D. Bible teaching:

    1. Matt. 8:14; 1 Cor. 9:5. Catholic argument that Peter divorced his wife falls in 1 Cor. 9:5. Paul says he was "leading her about."

    2. The teaching in 1 Cor. 7 was in view of "the present distress" (v. 26). Note that v. 9 applies to *all* unmarried people!

    3. Gen. 2:18 is as true today as it was in the beginning.

    4. Note 1 Tim. 5:14. The Catholic Church commands certain women not to marry.

    5. In the Lord's church, a bishop *must*:

      a. Be married (1 Tim. 3:2).

      b. Have children (1 Tim. 3:4). Note: The Lord's church and the Catholic Church are two different bodies. *Christ* rules His (Col. 1:18).

  II. **The Sacraments.**

    A. "A sacrament is an outward sign instituted by Christ to give grace....The sacrament gives the grace, which it signifies, by some inherent power attached to the outward sign by Christ Himself, or as theologians say, *ex operato*, that is, by performing the work which Christ has instituted" (*Question Box*, p. 747).

    B. We notice each of the seven sacraments briefly:

      1. *Baptism*.

        a. Children must be "baptized" (because they are "born in sin "The teaching of the church is simply this: Baptism is necessary for children as well as for adults, in order that they may be saved." "Every child born into this world has the guilt of original sin upon its soul ... Original sin excludes from heaven unless forgiven. It is forgiven only by baptism. Hence when an unbaptized child dies it cannot enter the kingdom of heaven....The soul of the child will not go to heaven, it is true; but neither will it go to a place of torments; it will go to what is called limbo of infants" (*Ibid.*, pp. 1, 5).

        b. Baptism can either be by pouring or immersion. "Catholic teaching is that baptism both by pouring and by immersion is valid.... In former times baptism by immersion was very common in the Holy Church; but in the course of centuries baptism by pouring has become the common practice because it obviates numerous inconveniences" (*Ibid.*, p. 4). Note the change and the reason for changing!

        c. Baptism of desire can replace water baptism. "This brings us to the important point of baptism of desire. In case of necessity this baptism will suffice for salvation" (*Ibid.*, p. 2).

        d. Bible teaching on these points:

          (1) Matt. 18:3; 19:14; 1 Jn. 3:4.

          (2) Rom. 6:3-4; Col. 2:12. By their own admission the word "baptize" is from a Greek word meaning "to dip into water" (*Ibid.*, p. 4).

          (3) Mk. 16:16; Acts 2:38; 22:16; 1 Pet. 3:21.

      2. *Confirmation*.

        a. Catholics admit that this "sacrament" has no basis in Scripture. "It is not easy to decide when this Sacrament was instituted by our Lord, as Holy Writ does not clearly state it" (*Ibid.*, p. 712).

        b. This "sacrament" is defined thus: "A sacrament of the New Law in which a baptized person receives the Holy Ghost, is strengthened in grace and signed and sealed as a soldier of Jesus Christ. The minister in the Latin rite anoints with Chrism and imposes hands, saying, 'I sign thee with the sign of the cross and confirm thee with the Chrism of salvation, in the name of the Father, and of the Son,

**Notes**

3. *Holy Eucharist.*
   a. "A sacrament of the New Law in which, under the appearances of bread and wine, the Body and Blood of Christ are truly, really and substantially present, as the grace-producing food of our souls. Moreover, 'it is very true that as much is contained under either species as under both; for Christ, whole and entire, exists under the species of bread, and under each particle of that species; and whole under species of wine, and under its separate parts'" (*Ibid.*, p. 186).
   b. Bible teaching:
      (1) Jesus was alive when the Lord's Supper was instituted (Matt. 26:26-30).
      (2) "This is my body ... my blood" is figurative language. (See Jn. 10:9-11; 15:5. Was Jesus a literal door, shepherd, and vine?)
      (3) 1 Cor. 11:23-34. These Christians were eating bread and drinking the *cup* (v. 26) in *memory* of Jesus' body and blood (vv. 24-25).
   c. Beginning in 1415 (Council of Constance) the cup was withheld from the "laity" (see Mk. 14:23). Those who have attended a Catholic service more recently know this has been changed.
4. Penance.
   a. "After hearing a penitent's confession and before giving him absolution, a confessor (priest) must impose a penance. While such a penance rarely nowadays bears any real relation to the gravity of the sins confessed, it must be in some sense proportionate thereto" (*Ibid.*, p. 397).
   b. Bible teaching:
      (1) Repentance (change of mind about sin) is commanded in the New Testament but penance is unheard of.
      (2) Luke 13:1-5; Acts 2:38; 3:19; 17:30; 8:22.
5. *Extreme Unction.*
   a. "A sacrament of the New Law in which, by anointing with oil and the prayers of the priest, health of soul and (sometimes) of body is conferred on a baptized person who is in danger of death through sickness" (*Ibid.*, p. 194).
   b. James 5:14-15 is given as Bible authority. These elders of James 5 were married men (Tit. 1:5-6); they were not unmarried priests in the Roman Catholic Church.
   c. Each church in New Testament days had a plurality of elders. So, "call for the *elders* (plural) of the church."
   d. These elders may have had the hands of the apostles laid on them (Acts 8:17-18) and thus able to perform the miracle of healing (1 Cor. 12:9).
6. *Holy Orders.*
   a. "A sacrament by which bishops, priests, and other ministers of the Church are ordained and receive the power and grace to perform their sacred duties. In addition to the effects of sanctifying grace and sacramental grace, this Sacrament likewise imprints an indelible character upon the soul. Hence, one who is validly ordained priest cannot be deprived of his priesthood even though he can be suspended from the exercise thereof; nor can he by his own free will, by heresy or apostasy, for example, lose the character imprinted on his soul" (*The Question Box*, pp. 469, 470).
   b. By this "sacrament" a "layman" is changed into a "clergyman." Now he has the power to bless anyone or anything, rule the flock, and administer the "sacraments" and forgive sins!
   c. The Roman Catholic Clergy claims to possess powers even the

*Catholic Dogmas (2)*

Lord's apostles never possessed.

7.  *Matrimony.*

   a.  "The Sacrament of Matrimony is a contract between a man and a woman both of whom are baptized and free to enter into the contract, to live together for the purpose of begetting and rearing children and of cherishing one another in a common life." "The marriages of the unbaptized are not sacrament" (*Catholic Dictionary*, p. 333).

   b.  In the past if a non-Catholic were to marry a Catholic, the Catholic Church required the non-Catholic to sign the following "pre-nuptial contract":

   I, the undersigned, not a member of the Catholic Church, wishing to contract marriage with the Catholic party whose signature is also affixed to this mutual agreement, being of sound mind and perfectly free, and only after understanding fully the import of my action, do hereby enter into this mutual agreement, understanding the execution of this agreement and the promises therein contained are made in contemplation of and in consideration for the consent, marriage, and consequent change of status of the hereinafter mentioned Catholic party, and I, therefore, hereby agree:

   1.  That I will not interfere in the least with the free exercise of the Catholic party's religion;
   2.  That I will adhere to the doctrine of the sacred indissolubility of the marriage bond, so that I cannot contract a second marriage while my consort is still alive, even though a civil divorce may have been obtained;
   3.  That all the children, both boys and girls, that may be born in this union shall be baptized and educated solely in the faith of the Roman Catholic Church, even in the event of the death of my Catholic consort. In case of dispute, I furthermore hereby agree fully that the custody of all children shall be given to such guardians as assure the faithful execution of this covenant and promise in the event that I cannot fulfill it myself;
   4.  That I will lead a married life in conformity with the teachings of the Catholic Church regarding birth control, realizing fully the attitude of the Catholic Church in this regard;
   5.  That no other marriage ceremony will take place before or after this ceremony by the Catholic priest.

   In testimony of which agreement, I do hereby solemnly swear that I will observe the above agreement and faithfully execute the promises therein contained, and do now affix my signature in approval thereof.

   _____
   (Signature of non-Catholic party)

   c.  Some time back an article appeared in the newspaper entitled, "Pope Eases Marriage Bans." "The non-Catholic partner to a mixed marriage *still must be asked* to promise to place no obstacle in the way of education of children in the Roman Catholic faith. If, however, the non-Catholic advances serious objections of conscience, the Bishop is instructed to refer the case to the Holy See for judgment. The intention is expressed to rule on such cases in Rome in the 'most fervid sense of charity'" (Emphasis mine, A.M.). Not much "ease" here! "In ordinary circumstances, both Catholic and non-Catholic partners should make their pledges with regard to children in writing, as in the past. But the local bishop is authorized to eliminate this requirement and to rule on whether reference to it should be made in the marriage contract."

    d.  On October 31, 1979, I called the priest at the Catholic Church meeting at 1041 Central Ave., Knoxville, TN, and he gave me the following information concerning the requirements for a non-Catholic to marry a Catholic:

        (1)  The non-Catholic must be free to marry – that is, not divorced.

        (2)  The non-Catholic must agree not to interfere in any way with the Catholic's religion.

        (3)  The non-Catholic must have five or six (four months, another priest said) meetings with the priest prior to the ceremony.

        (4)  The Catholic party must sign a paper agreeing that the children born to the union will be brought up in the Catholic religion, and that all the children born to the union will baptized as infants.

        (5)  When the Catholic party signs these papers, the non-Catholic party must be present and thus agree to the stipulations.

        (6)  The marriage must be performed by a Catholic priest.

## III. Purgatory.

    A.  "The place and state in which souls suffer for a while and are purged (thus the name "purgatory") after death, before they go to heaven, on account of their sins" (*Catholic Dictionary*, p. 437).

    B.  This unscriptural doctrine has encouraged other Catholic promotions:

        1.  Indulgences (the remission of the temporal punishment due to those sins of which the guilt has been forgiven).

        2.  Enlisted people to engage in Crusades.

        3.  Contributed to extermination of heretics.

        4.  Used to raise money to build cathedrals.

    C.  Bible teaching: Heb. 9:27-28; Rev. 22:10-12; Eccl. 12:7.

## IV. Veneration of Relics.

    A.  "The corpse of a saint or any part thereof; any part of his clothing anything intimately connected with him. The veneration of relics can be traced at least to the middle of the 2nd century and was regulated by the Council of Trent, which directed that no new relics should be admitted without episcopal authentication" (*Ibid.*, p. 448).

    B.  It is said that Rome has the comb of the rooster that crowed for Peter, bones of the apostles, wood from the cross, etc.

    C.  This is grounded in heathenism and superstition – not divine authority.

## V. Images.

    A.  "The images especially of Christ, of the Virgin Mother of God, and of other saints, are to be had and kept in churches and due honor and reverence paid to them; not because it is believed that there is any divinity or power in them or that anything may be asked from them, or that any faith may be put in them. or that anything may be asked for them ... but because the honor shown to them is referred to the prototypes which they represent; so that through these images which we kiss and before which we bow with bared heads, we worship Christ and honor the saints whose likeness they display" (Council of Trent).

    B.  Joe Malone, in "Why I Left the Catholic Church" (p. 219) states: "*Life Magazine*, reporting the ceremonies in Ottawa, Canada, in June, 1947, at the Marian Congress, pointed out that a great procession of devout people knelt and kissed the foot of the giant statue of Mary 'until the paint wore off its toes.'"

    C.  Bible teaching.

        1.  Exod. 20:4-5; Rom. 1:21-25; Acts 17:29-30.

        2.  What about pictures of Jesus today?

            a.  Who knows what He looked like?

            b.  Did He have long hair (1 Cor. 11:14)?

c.  Jesus left us what He wanted us to have to remind us of Him (Lk. 22:19-20). Are the Lord's arrangements sufficient?

**VI. Maryolatry.**

A.  Three basic false assumptions:

1.  Immaculate Conception. "By authority of our Lord Jesus Christ, of the blessed apostles Peter and Paul, and by our own authority, we declare, pronounce, and define that the doctrine which holds that the most Blessed Virgin Mary, in the first instance of her conception, by a special grace and privilege of the Almighty God, in view of the merits of Jesus Christ, the Saviour of mankind, was preserved free from the stain of all original sin, has been revealed by God, and therefore is to be firmly and steadfastly believed by all the faithful" (*Ex cathedra* declaration of Pope Pius IX, December 8, 1854).

    a.  This false doctrine was invented to escape the consequences of the false doctrine of hereditary total depravity.

    b.  See Matt. 18:3; 19:14; Ezek. 18:19-20.

2.  Perpetual Virginity. "It is also of Catholic faith that our Lady remained a virgin throughout her life" (*Catholic Dictionary*, p. 548). See Matt. 1:24-25; 13:55-56.

3.  Bodily Assumption.

    a.  Made an official dogma November 1, 1950.

    b.  "The modern movement to have the belief included as Catholic Dogma was started in 1863 when Isabella II, queen of Spain, asked Pope Pius IX for a papal ruling on the matter. Catholic belief in the bodily assumption is based on the statement of Saint John of Damascus, born about 676, that her tomb, when opened upon the request of Saint Thomas, was found empty and the apostles therefore concluded that the body was taken up to heaven" (from a Vatican news release carried in the newspaper in the fall of 1950).

B.  Mary is called the "Mother of God." Prayers are made to her.

1.  "Mary is the Mother of Jesus, Jesus is God, therefore she is the Mother of God....Mary is the spiritual mother of all living; Catholics venerate her with an honor above that accorded to other saints, but differently from the divine worship given to God only; they pray to her, and she in heaven intercedes with her Son, God the Son, for them" (*Catholic Dictionary*, p. 329).

2.  See 1 Tim. 2:5 and Jn. 14:14. Jesus is the only mediator and prayer is to be made to God in the name of Jesus Christ!

3.  No special honor is accorded her in the New Testament. See Lk. 11:27-28. The Lord honors people for their obedience to his teaching!

**Conclusion:**

1.  These teachings only scratch the surface of Roman Catholic dogmas.

2.  These help us to see how far men can go away from God when once they begin to delve into human wisdom.

3.  We love our Catholic friends and neighbors and trust that these lessons will better equip us to help them return to the truth that will free from sin.

## Short Answer

1. What does the word "celibacy" mean? _____

   _____

2. Make a list of some Bible passages that teach it is right to marry. _____

   _____

3. Where in the New Testament does it say that some would "forbid to marry"?

   _____

4. Is it right to refer to the Lord's Supper as a "sacrament"? _____

5. Make a list of the dangers involved in a Christian marrying a Catholic. _____

   _____

   _____

6. Be prepared to discuss the differences between Bible teaching about "hades" and the Catholic doctrine of "purgatory" (see Lk. 16:19-31; Acts 2:25-32; Rev. 20:11-15). _____

   _____

7. What has the Lord left to help us remember His Son? _____

   _____

8. Does the New Testament teach that Mary remained a virgin all of her life? _____ If your answer is "no," what is your proof? _____

   _____

9. In Matthew 12, who did Jesus say his brothers, sisters, and mother were?

   _____

   _____

10. Concerning baptism, answer these questions:
    a. Who can be baptized? _____
    b. Why be baptized? _____
    c. How is baptism performed? _____
    d. Where (creek, pond, etc.)? _____

## Underline

1. Peter was a (married, divorced, single) man.
2. One of the qualifications of a bishop is that he must have (grandchildren, nephews, children).
3. The Catholic Church has (5, 7, 9) "sacraments."
4. The Bible teaches that (purgatory, annihilation, judgment) follows death.
5. (Jesus, Mary, Peter) is the mediator between God and man.

## Matching

| | | | |
|---|---|---|---|
| _____ | 1. Genesis 2:18 | A. | Burial in baptism |
| _____ | 2. Colossians 2:12 | B. | Lord's Supper |
| _____ | 3. Luke 13:1-5 | C. | Idols condemned |
| _____ | 4. Acts 17:29 | D. | Not good that man should be alone |
| _____ | 5. 1 Corinthians 11:23-34 | E. | Repent or perish |

## Lesson 6
# Reformation (1)

**Introduction:**

I.   In our lessons thus far, we have studied the establishment of the Lord's church; its growth, departures from the divine pattern, the rise of the Catholic Church, and some doctrines of Catholicism.

II.  As the years rolled by, the Roman Catholic Church became more powerful and more corrupt. In this period from the 5th to the 15th centuries:

    A.  The Bible became virtually a sealed book. "The Bible was chained to the pulpit."

    B.  Priest-ridden people were kept in ignorance.

III. As time went on, there were courageous voices raised against the corruption of Rome. These voices, protesting the excesses of Catholicism, eventually produced the "Protestant Reformation."

**Discussion:**

I.  **The Underlying Causes of the Reformation.**

    A.  *Corruption within the Catholic Church.*

        1.  Wicked popes.

            a.  *The Catholic Question Box* (pp. 483-4) readily admits that there were a "few unworthy popes."

            b.  John XII was such a monster of wickedness that upon the complaint of the people of Rome, the emperor Otho caused him to be tried and deposed. The Pope's reply was, "We hear that you want to make another pope. If that is your design, I excommunicate you all in the name of the Almighty, that you may not have it in your power to ordain any other, or even to celebrate mass."

            c.  Benedict IX (1033) was more than once expelled from Rome by the people for his debaucheries, and finally sold his popedom to Gregory VI.

            d.  Alexander VI (1492) was elected through bribery, and history reveals no example of depravity that exceeds that of this "head of the church." It is said that not one of the analysts of the Roman Church has breathed a whisper in his praise. Among his debaucheries, he is said to have given a splendid entertainment in the Vatican to no less than 50 public prostitutes. Although popes never marry, this link in the "apostolic chain" is said to have acknowledged five children by a Roman matron.

        2.  Indulgences.

            a.  An indulgence was a document that could be bought for a sum of money and that would free one from the temporal penalty of sin.

            b.  During the dark ages, indulgences became a license to sin.

            c.  John Tetzel was the most notorious indulgence salesman.

    B.  *Internal strife.*

        1.  Division between the East and the West (1054).

            a.  When Constantine moved his capitol to Constantinople in 330, he paved the way for the separation of the Catholic Church into the East and West.

            b.  Difficulty arose over the use of the title "universal bishop."

    c.  Then the two movements got at odds over:
      (1)  When to celebrate Easter.
      (2)  Celibacy. Priests in the Eastern church marry.
      (3)  Bowing before relics, pictures, etc. The Catholic Church in the East removed all crosses from their buildings so they could not be charged with idolatry.
    d.  In 1053 the patriarch of Constantinople condemned the church in the West for the use of unleavened bread in communion. After prolonged discussions, the patriarch was excommunicated. The patriarch was not to be outdone so he excommunicated the pope of Rome. From this time (1054) the Roman Catholic and the Greek Orthodox churches were separate.

  2.  "Babylonian Captivity."
    a.  Early in the 14th century, a French archbishop was chosen pope due to a struggle over the right of kings to tax clergy and wage war. The headquarters of the Roman Church were moved to Avignon, France.
    b.  In 1377 the papacy was moved back to Rome and Urban VI was elected pope. He didn't get along with the hierarchy, so they elected another pope, Clement VII, who moved the church capitol back to Avignon. But Urban VI continued to reign in Rome. Both popes claimed to be the legitimate successors of Peter and this split, referred to as "The Great Schism," continued into the 15th century when the Council of Pisa (1409) deposed both the Avignon and Roman popes and appointed a third. The other popes refused to recognize this action and so for a while there were three rival popes. The Council of Constance (1414-1418) resulted in the elimination of all three and the election of one new pope – Martin V.

C.  *The Inquisition.*
  1.  The Inquisition was an elaborate system of the Catholic Church to inquire into the beliefs of persons suspected of being heretics. People accused of being heretics were tried in the court of the Inquisition. If an accused person confessed and renounced his heresy he was reconciled with the Church on performance of penance. If he did not voluntarily confess, he would be subjected to torture, one of the most commonly used forms being the rack, which wrenched the legs of the victim. If torture failed to make the victim confess he was declared a heretic and turned over to the secular authorities to be burned at the stake.
  2.  The Inquisition existed from 1229 to 1834 and operated chiefly in Spain, Portugal, Italy, and France. Thousands were put to death because they dared differ with the Roman Catholic Church. In France, 930 Inquisitional sentences from 1308 to 1323 (15 years) show that 42 were put to death, 140 acquitted, and 748 were tortured.

## II. Other Factors That Contributed to the Reformation:

A.  *The Renaissance – the re-birth of desire for learning.*
B.  *Translation of the Bible into different languages* so that the man in the street could read it.
C.  *Invention of the printing press* by Gutenburg in 1454.
  1.  Prior to this, all books, including the Bible, were written by hand.
  2.  This made the price so high and the supply so limited that the common man could not afford to own any books – not even the Bible.

## III. Forerunners of the Reformation:

A.  *Between 1000 and 1400 different groups arose* as internal and external revolts to purify religion. Among them were:
  1.  The Albigenses.

# Notes

a. They rejected the authority of the Roman Catholic Church. They put emphasis on the authority of the New Testament.

b. In 1208, a Roman Catholic Crusade was sponsored in an effort to wipe them out.

c. Not until the end of the 14th century was the Inquisition able to destroy them.

2. Waldenses.

a. A Puritan movement named after Peter Waldo.

b. Attempted to reinstate the Bible as authority.

c. The Roman Catholic Church reacted to this movement by excommunication, by forbidding the people to use Bible translations in their own tongue, and by the Inquisition.

B. *Peter Du Bruys, France.*

1. He contended for New Testament authority.

2. He opposed infant baptism, transubstantiation, etc.

3. He was burned at the stake in 1126.

C. *John Wycliff (1320-1384), England. "Morning star of the Reformation."*

1. "He anticipated the grand Reformation with a knowledge of the religious situations, with a perspicuity of genius, and by apostolic blows of radical reform, that shook the very foundations of the papal edifice."

2. He set aside Papal decrees by a direct appeal to the Word of God.

3. He denied transubstantiation, confirmation, extreme unction, auricular confession, indulgences.

4. He boldly asserted that presbyters and bishops were the same in the New Testament.

5. He translated most of the Bible into the English language.

6. He was excommunicated by the Catholic Church but he was allowed to die a natural death.

7. Some years after his death, pope Martin V had his bones dug up, burned, and the ashes thrown in the River Swift. "The vicious spirit of apostasy would not let his bones rest in peace!"

D. *John Huss (1369-1415), Bohemia.*

1. Born of poor peasants – received a good education. Rose to the position of dean of the theological faculty of the University of Prague.

2. Came to appreciate the writings of Wycliff. "I am attracted to his writings, for all his efforts are to lead men back to the law of Christ."

3. Pope then decreed that no one in the University could hold the doctrines of Wycliff. Huss continued his teaching in the chapel. He was then excommunicated.

4. He remained in the city and taught. Then the city was placed under interdict. Huss could not be harbored or fed. No priest could perform his duties in the city until Huss was expelled.

5. Huss then left the city but continued to preach in the country.

6. The Council of Constance (1414-18) brought him to trial. He was promised safe conduct and was supposed to be allowed to defend himself. His trial was a farce.

7. On his birthday, July 6, 1415, Huss calmly heard his sentence.

8. His priestly garments were ripped off, a miter of paper was placed on his head with this inscription, "A Ringleader of Heretics."

9. His books were burned at the gate of the church and he was led to the suburbs to be burned alive.

10. As the flames leaped about him, he sang a hymn and then cried, "Jesus Christ, thou Son of the living God, have mercy on me."

11. His ashes were then collected and thrown in the Rhine.

## Conclusion:

1. Every movement of any consequence has had a foundation on which to build.

2. The Reformation was motivated by the corruption within the Roman

**John Wycliff (1328-1384)**

**John Huss (1373-1415)**

Catholic Church.

3. The ground work was laid in renewed desire on the part of people to learn; in the invention of the printing press; and in the translation, publication, and distribution of the Word of God.
4. But there had to be *people*; people who loved *truth* more than life!
5. There were men like Wycliff and Huss, but just as importantly, there were that host of common folk who wanted to know the truth and were willing to pay the price.
6. What kind of a person would you have been if you had lived back *then*?
7. What kind of a person are you *now*? Are you concerned about *truth*? Are you willing to pay whatever price is demanded in order to obey the Lord's will?

# Questions

**Supply the Missing Word**

1. A Catholic license to sin. _____
2. According to 2 Timothy 2:15, what each individual is to do. _____
3. Place where the Bible was "chained." _____
4. Catholic system of trying "heretics." _____
5. Morning star of the Reformation. _____

**True or False**

_____ 1. The Catholic Church has always been, and remains, a united group.
_____ 2. Ephesians 4:4-6 teaches there is one body (church).
_____ 3. The invention of the printing press contributed to an increased knowledge of the Word of God.
_____ 4. John 8:32 teaches that truth enslaves.
_____ 5. Jesus, in His prayer (John 17), affirmed that God's word is truth.

**Short Answer**

1. Do you think the Bible can be understood by "common" people (see Eph. 3:4)? _____
2. What, would you say, is the greatest threat to the purity and faithfulness of the Lord's church today? _____
   _____
3. For what, according to 2 Timothy 3:16-17, is Scripture profitable? _____
   _____
4. Do you think elevating men has been a problem from the beginning of the church (see 1 Cor. 3:1-7)? _____
5. Would you say that a majority of denominational bodies today stress individual study of God's Word? _____
6. Is there danger, do you think, of putting too much importance on a "local" preacher? _____
7. Why is a study of church history important to us? _____
   _____
8. From your study of church history thus far, list some blessings you have that some in years past did not have. _____
   _____
9. What should be a Christian's attitude toward those with whom he differs?
   _____
10. According to Proverbs 23:23, what should a person do about truth? _____
    _____

## Lesson 7
# Reformation (2)

**Introduction:**
I.   In the last lesson we gave attention to the factors and people that were responsible (at least in part) for the reformation:
  A.   Corruption within the Roman Catholic Church.
    1.   Wicked popes.
    2.   Internal strife.
    3.   The Inquisition Courts.
  B.   External factors:
    1.   The Renaissance.
    2.   Bible translations.
    3.   Invention of the printing press.
  C.   People:
    1.   Albigenses.
    2.   Waldenses.
    3.   John Wycliff – "Morning Star of the Reformation."
    4.   John Huss.
II.   In this lesson, we notice the formation of the first Protestant denomination and some general things about the reformation.
  A.   It needs to be pointed out that the men involved in the Reformation did not intend to begin new churches.
  B.   The aim of these men was to reform the Roman Catholic Church.
    1.   Heb. 6:1-6 is speaking of individual apostasy; however, the principle might be applied to the situation under discussion. The writer said, "It is impossible to renew them again to repentance."
    2.   The Roman Catholic Church had gone too far to be reformed.
    3.   Viewed from this standpoint, the Reformation was a failure. But good, as well as evil and error, came out of it as we shall see.

**Martin Luther (1483-1546)**

**Discussion:**
I.   **Luther's Experiences (1483-1546).**
  A.   *Son of a poor miner but was given a good education.*
    1.   In higher education he began a study of law.
    2.   In 1505 the death of a close friend caused Luther to enter the Augustinian monastery at Erfurt.
    3.   In 1507 he was ordained a priest and assigned to Whittenburg, Germany.
  B.   *Luther then began a serious investigation of the Bible – his troubles began.*
    1.   In 1512 he was awarded a Doctor of Theology degree and began lecturing at the University.
    2.   About this time he was sent to Rome on a special mission and the corruption he saw helped crystallize his convictions.

II.   **Luther's Break With the Roman Catholic Church.**
  A.   *John Tetzel came into Germany selling indulgences.*
    1.   Luther preached against such and on October 31, 1517, nailed his 95 theses to the church door of All-Saints church in Whittenburg.

2. Luther did this, not to fight against the Catholic Church, but to preserve the honor of the church.
3. Copies of the propositions spread all over Germany and Luther's name became a household word.

B. *Out of this, John Eck branded Luther as a heretic.*
1. This led to a 23 day debate between Luther and Eck. Eck's purpose was to draw Luther out enough on his doctrines so that the Pope could be persuaded to excommunicate him. Eck was successful.
2. The Papal bull of condemnation was then issued against Luther. When it was delivered to Luther, he made a public display of burning it on the streets of Whittenburg. He was then excommunicated.

C. *In April 1521, Luther was summoned to appear before the Diet of Worms.*
1. Before this tribunal he was offered the opportunity to recant. His reply was: "Unless I shall be convinced by the testimonies of the Scriptures or by clear reason,... I neither can nor will make any retraction, since it is neither safe nor honorable to act against conscience; I can naught else! Here I stand! God help me!"
2. On May 25, he was declared an outlaw.
3. As he returned to Whittenburg, his friends "kidnapped" him and for about a year he remained in Wartburg Castle.
4. During this time he translated the New Testament into the German language.

III. **Formation of the Lutheran Church.**
A. *As an outgrowth of all these events, groups of people began to meet together who were in sympathy with Luther's teaching.*
1. The movement was given added direction by Luther with his publication of two catechisms in 1529.
2. In 1530 Philip Melanchthon published the *Augsburg Confession* which helped form the doctrinal foundation of the Lutheran Church.
3. Lutherans hold to the so-called Apostles', Nicene, and Athanasian Creeds.

B. *Interesting facts about the Lutheran Church.*
1. Doctrines.
   a. Two Sacraments – baptism and the Lord's Supper ("sacrament" unscriptural).
   b. Baptism is "by washing, pouring, immersion, and sprinkling" (Col. 2:12; Rom. 6:4).
   c. Infants born totally depraved; therefore must be "baptized" (Ezek. 18:20; Matt. 18:3; 19:14).
   d. The body and blood of Christ are "in, with and under the bread and wine of the Supper" (this is close to the transubstantiation doctrine of the Catholic Church).
   e. Direct operation of the Holy Spirit on the heart of the sinner; faith is "wholly and solely the gift and work of God"; salvation is by faith *alone* (Mk. 16:15-16; Rom. 1:16; 10:17; Jas. 2:24).
2. Organization.
   a. Locally – congregationally governed by a "church council" consisting of the "pastor" and elected "lay officers."
   b. Synod is the next higher body, composed of "Pastors" and "lay representatives" elected by the congregations.
   c. Highest level of Lutheran government is the general body. It may be national or even international and meets annually, biennially, or triennially.
   d. See Acts 20:28; 1 Pet. 5:1-3; Heb. 13:17; Eph. 4:11; Phil. 1:1.
3. Division.
   a. At one time there were no fewer than 150 different Lutheran bodies in this country.
   b. Today that number has been reduced to less than 20.

IV. **Fundamental Principles on Which the Reformation Movement Was Based.**
   A. *The Bible was accepted as the only rule of faith and practice.*
      1. This was in opposition to the Catholic position that tradition is equal in authority with the written Word.
      2. This position, if it had been completely believed and respected, would have resulted in the restoration of the Lord's church instead of the establishment of Protestant Denominations.
      3. But this truth was modified (its power destroyed) by the following:
   B. *"What is not contrary to Scripture is for Scripture and Scripture for it."*
      1. These are Luther's words and the idea remains an important one in all Protestant Denominations.
      2. Simply stated, it says that anything may be accepted in religion which does not expressly contradict the Scriptures!
      3. When Luther left the Catholic Church, he carried many false teachings with him such as instrumental music and sprinkling.
      4. He, and other reformers, justified their unscriptural practices by this appeal to the silence of the Scriptures.
      5. How many volumes would it have taken for the Lord to have included every specific prohibition? How many catalogs would Sears have to publish to list all the prices they are not asking for the items they sell? How many woods did God tell Noah not to use? Can we put steak and coke on the Lord's table? When you send your child to the grocery, do you put on your list all the things he is not to purchase or the items you want?
   C. *The doctrine of justification by faith only.*
      1. This extreme was produced by the Catholic doctrine of salvation by faith and works of human merit.
      2. God's order, from Adam down to the close of the last New Testament book, is this:
         • Man believes (through the evidence God provides)
         • God commands
         • Man obeys
         • God blesses
   D. *The principle of the priesthood of all believers.*
      1. This was in contrast to the special priesthood of the Roman Catholic system.
      2. When carried to its logical end, this would destroy:
         a. Infallibility of the pope.
         b. The special powers of the Cardinals and all other Catholic officials.
         c. Auricular Confession.
         d. "Ordained officials" baptizing, serving the Lord's Supper, etc.
      3. See 1 Peter 2:5, 9.
   E. *The removal of obstructions placed between the believer and Christ.*
      1. This does away with intercession of saints, praying to Mary, veneration of relics and images, etc.
      2. 1 Timothy 2:5; John 14:6.

**Conclusion:**
   1. People reared in the 20th century have problems just as those people did who lived back in the 16th century.
   2. With all the religious confusion about me, *what should I believe? Whose doctrine should I follow? What church should I join?*
   3. The answer is as simple as the truth taught in 2 Timothy 3:16-17: "All Scripture is given by inspiration of God, and is profitable for doctrine, for reproof, for correction, for instruction in righteousness: that the man of God may be perfect, throughly furnished unto all good works."

a. Believe nothing but God's Word – it alone is inspired!
b. Follow no teaching but Christ's – He has all authority (Matt. 28:18)!
c. Join no church! The church is God's house or God's family (1 Tim. 3:15). You don't join a family; you are born into it (Jn. 3:1-7).
d. Obey the gospel of Christ – the Lord will save you and add you to His church (Rom. 6:17-18; Acts 2:36-47; Heb. 5:8-9; 1 Pet. 4:17).

4. Remember that the decision you make will face you at the judgment!

## Questions

**Matching**

| | | | |
|---|---|---|---|
| _____ | 1. Protestant denominations | A. | Ezekiel 18:20; 1 John 3:4 |
| _____ | 2. Protest | B. | Something handed down |
| _____ | 3. All Christians | C. | Key ingredient in Protestation |
| _____ | 4. Sin not inherited | D. | Reformation produced |
| _____ | 5. Tradition | E. | Priests (1 Pet. 2:5) |

**Short Answer**

1. Were those men involved in the Reformation successful in reforming the Catholic Church? _____

2. Do you think we owe any gratitude to men such as Huss, Wycliff, and Luther? _____

3. Where, in the book of James, are we told that salvation is not by faith alone? _____

4. Does the Holy Spirit operate on the heart of man in conversion?_____
If your answer is "yes" can you explain how? _____
_____

5. What would you teach a person who wanted to put Coca Cola and potatoes on the Lord's Table?_____
_____

6. Does the silence of the Scriptures give consent?_____
If not, why not? _____

7. Does the Bible teach that you can "join" the church of Christ?_____
If not, how does a person become a part of the church? _____
_____

8. Make a list of the things wrong with the Lutheran Church. _____
_____
_____

9. Did Luther begin his religious life as a Lutheran or a Catholic? _____

10. Can debating be a useful tool in arriving at the truth? _____

**Suggest the Basic Truth in Each Passage**

1. 2 Peter 2:20-22 _____
2. Col. 2:12 _____
3. Rom. 1:16 _____
4. Philippians 1:1_____
5. John 17:20-21 _____

## Lesson 8
# Church of England

**Introduction:**

I. This is the third lesson dealing with attempts to reform the Roman Catholic Church.

    A. We have observed that these attempts failed.

    B. Out of Luther's work reformation did not come; rather, a new religious body was born.

    C. This period, instead of being a reformation period, was a period of Protestant denominational births.

II. In the last lesson we noticed five fundamental bases on which the reformation was begun:

    A. Bible – only rule of faith and practice.

    B. Anything may be accepted in religion that is not expressly forbidden.

    C. Justification by faith only.

    D. Priesthood of all believers.

    E. Removal of obstructions between man and Christ.

III. Reformatory efforts were not confined to Germany. In this lesson we give attention to the work and results of another man.

**Discussion:**

I. **Reformation Activity in England.**

    A. *Principles of the Lutheran reformation swept across the English Channel.*

       1. The English people had some preparation – John Wycliff and others less well known had taught against fundamental Catholic doctrines.

       2. Catholic corruption had left a bad taste in people's mouths – they were ready for changes to be made. English people loved their freedom.

       3. But when the break with Catholicism came, it was more political and social than religious.

    B. *Henry VIII ruled England from 1509 to 1547.*

       1. He was devoted to the Catholic Church.

       2. In 1521, Pope Leo X gave Henry the title "Defender of the Faith" for his defense of the sacramental system against the writings of Luther.

II. **Henry VIII Had Marriage Problems.**

    A. *Henry was married to Catherine of Aragon.* (She was the daughter of Ferdinand and Isabella of Spain.)

       1. Henry claimed he never loved her (she was the widow of his brother).

       2. She bore him six children but only one daughter survived (Mary).

       3. He argued that he ought to have a son to succeed him.

       4. He happened to be in love with an attendant in the Queen's court – Anne Boleyn.

    B. *Henry requested permission of the Pope to divorce Catherine and marry Anne.*

       1. The Pope refused the request.

       2. Henry then divorced Catherine and married Anne in 1533.

       3. The Pope excommunicated Henry in 1534.

III. **The Beginning of the Church of England.**

    A. *Later in the same year (1534) Henry proclaimed himself the head of the*

*Catholic Church in England.*
  1. Shortly thereafter he was able to get the English Parliament to make the act official by cutting off the English Church from Rome and declaring the English Sovereign (king or queen) head of the church. This was known as the *Act of Supremacy.*
  2. The Catholic Church in England then had its name changed to the Anglican Church or the Church of England.
  3. There were some changes in doctrine and practice, but in the main it was simply a Catholic Church under English rule. This organization still is nearer the Catholic system than any other Protestant body.
  B. *Though the initial break with Catholicism was not doctrinal, Henry VIII drafted Ten Articles in 1536.* They have been summarized thus:

  "The authoritative standards of faith are the Bible, the Apostles', Nicene, and Athanasian creeds, and the 'four first councils.' Only three sacraments are defined: baptism, penance, and the Lord's Supper; the others are not mentioned in approval or denial. Justification implies faith in Christ alone, but confession and absolution and works of charity are also necessary. Christ is physically present in the supper. Images are to the honored but with moderation. The saints are to be invoked, but not because they 'will hear us sooner than Christ.' Masses for the dead are desirable, but the idea that the 'bishop of Rome' can deliver out of purgatory is to be rejected."

  1. These articles were later enlarged into Forty-Two Articles.
  2. Revised in 1563 into *Thirty-Nine Articles*, these Articles have become the formal statement of faith for the Church of England.
  C. *Being born of social and political expediencies, trouble lay ahead.*
  1. Upon Henry's death in 1547, his son Edward, who had a Protestant mother, came to the throne and continued his father's work.
  2. At his death, "Bloody Mary," daughter of Henry and Catherine, ascended the throne.
      a. England then experienced a "Catholic Reaction."
      b. Mary probably had up to 400 people put to death who had opposed Catholicism.
  3. When Mary died, Elizabeth, daughter of Henry and Anne Boleyn, began to rule and she re-directed England toward Protestantism.

## IV. Interesting Things About the Church of England.
  A. *History in America.*
  1. First planted on the shores of America by Drake in California in 1578.
  2. The movement grew fast in the South and "West," but made little headway in the East for many years.
  3. The American Revolution almost destroyed the Church of England in America.
      a. Most of the clergy were loyal to the King of England.
      b. They fled back to England during the latter part of the war.
  4. In 1783, reorganization came and the name *Protestant Episcopal Church* was adopted.
  B. *Form of government.*
  1. Basic unit is the parish. It is overseen by the Rector (Priest).
  2. Wardens have charge of the church records and collection of alms.
  3. Vestrymen have charge of all church property.
  4. Parishes are grouped geographically into 74 dioceses. The dioceses elect the Bishops.
  5. Government in the diocese is vested in the Bishop and the diocesan convention, composed of clerical and lay members, which meet annually.
  6. Every three years there is a general convention composed of two houses – Bishops and deputies. Laws passed here must be submitted

**Henry VIII (1525-1533)**

to the dioceses for ratification before becoming law.
7. The ecclesiastical head of the Church is the Presiding Bishop elected by the general convention. He serves to age of retirement – 72.

C. *Doctrines.*
1. Children are born in sin; must be regenerated in baptism (*Book of Common Prayer*, pp. 273,274).
    a. Sin not inherited – it is committed (1 Jn. 3:4).
    b. Baptism is for those who can believe and repent (Mk. 16:15-16; Acts 2:38).
2. "That we are justified by faith only is a most wholesome doctrine and very full of comfort" (*Ibid.*, p. 605; see Jas. 2:24).
3. Jesus "died to reconcile His Father to us" (*Ibid.*, p. 603; see 2 Cor. 5:19-21).
4. "Baptism" can be performed either by pouring or immersion (*Ibid.*, p. 279; see Jn. 3:23; Matt. 3:16; Rom. 6:4).
5. Special days are observed (*Ibid.*, pp. L, LI [see Gal. 4:10-11))
6. Believe Ten Commandments still binding (*Ibid.*, p. 68; see Col 2:14; Heb. 10:9-10; 8:7-8).

**Conclusion:**
1. If you had been living at this point in our study, you would have had these choices before you:
    a. You could have submitted to the authority of the Pope of Rome, believed the doctrines of the Roman Catholic Church, and become a part of that religious denomination. But to do so you would have had to deny the authority of Christ and the all-sufficiency of the New Testament!
    b. You could have taken the other branch of Catholicism. You could have followed the Patriarch of Constantinople and become a member of the Greek Orthodox Catholic Church. But to do this would have demanded that you affiliate with and pledge support of doctrines contrary to the plain teachings of God's Word.
    c. You could have refused to be a part of either division of Catholicism and followed Luther to become a member of the Lutheran Church. But to do this would have put you in conflict with many simple and plain teachings of inspired men, not the least of which would have been 1 Corinthians 1:13: "Is Christ divided; was Paul crucified for you; or were you baptized in the name of Paul?" Did Luther have the God-given right to start another church?
    d. Or, you could have rejected this Protestant Body and joined the Catholic Church in England – ruled by the head of the British government. Could you have done this with a good conscience knowing that "we walk by faith and not by sight" (2 Cor. 5:7) and that "faith cometh by hearing and hearing by the Word of God" (Rom. 10:17)?
2. However, these are not the only choices you would have had – one remains:
    a. You could have taken the Bible and studied it for yourself (2 Tim. 2:15).
    b. You could then, upon your faith in the Lord, your repentance of your sins, and your confession of your faith in Christ, have been baptized into Christ unto the remission of sins (Mk. 16:15-16; Acts 2:38; 8:26-40; Gal. 3:26-27).
    c. You could have refused to have anything to do with any man-made religious organization.
    d. By your obedience from the heart your sins could have been washed away (Rom. 6:17-18; Acts 22:16).
    e. By your obedience you could have been added to the church by the Lord (Acts 2:47).
    f. There is only one body and that body is the church (Eph. 4:4; Col.

1:18).

  g. So now you have what you have been seeking – salvation from sin.

  h. You are a member of the church of Christ's choice.

  i. Why ruin the work of God by joining something the Bible never heard of?

  j. Why make your worship vain by upholding the doctrines of men (Matt. 15:9)?

 3. Why not go back of the corruptions of men to the pure Word of God – back of the churches of men to the church built by Christ (Matt. 16:18) and bought with His blood (Acts 20:28)?

# Questions

**Fill in the Blanks**

1. The Church of England is much like the _____ Church.

2. The Church of England had its origin through the efforts of _____ .

3. The founder of the Church of England lacked respect for Matthew ____:9.

4. In America, the Church of England is called the _____ Church.

5. According to Matthew 15:9, the doctrines of_____ make worship vain.

**True or False**

_____ 1. The "creed book" of the Lord's church is the Bible.

_____ 2. James 2 teaches we are justified by faith only.

_____ 3. Faith without works is dead.

_____ 4. "Bloody Mary" was a good woman who was misunderstood.

_____ 5. Mark 16:15-16 and Acts 2:38 indicate that little children can be baptized.

**Short Answer**

1. In Matthew 16:18 and 1 Thessalonians 1:1 the word "church" is use differently. Explain the difference._____

  _____

2. According to 1 Corinthians 12:13, into what is a person baptized? _____

3. Thus far we have studied the origin of Catholicism and two Protestant denominations. Which of these do you find in the New Testament?_____

4. Where in the New Testament do you find the qualifications for elders? _____

  _____

  Deacons?_____

5. What doctrine of the Church of England necessarily gives rise to the practice of infant baptism? _____

  _____

6. According to 1 Peter 5:1-4, what do elders feed and oversee?._____

  _____

7. How would you show that the Old Testament (including the Ten Commandments) are no longer binding? _____

8. How much authority does Christ (according to Matt. 28:18) have? _____

9. Where or how is that authority expressed?_____

10. According to Hebrews 8, Moses had a pattern for building the tabernacle. Is there a pattern for the work, worship, and organization of the Lord's church?

  _____

11. According to Matthew 15, what happens when the blind lead the blind?

  _____

**Notes**

## Lesson 9
# Presbyterian Church

### Introduction:
I. Thus far in our studies we have gone into Germany and England.
- A. In our last lesson we traced the development of the Church of England.
  1. Observed that it was produced more by political and social expediencies than by religious conviction.
  2. We took note of the fact that the Episcopal Church is more closely allied to Roman Catholicism than any other Protestant body.
- B. In this lesson we turn our attention to Switzerland and Scotland.
II. In this study, we shall see varying degrees of respect for Bible authority being manifested.

### Discussion:
I. **The work of Ulrich Zwingli (1482-1531).**
- A. *Born in German speaking Switzerland, village of Wildhaus.*
  1. Received a good education.
  2. In 1506 appointed a parish priest at Glarus.
  3. In 1518 appointed chief pastor in the Cathedral Church in Zurich.
- B. *By this time Zwingli had developed the idea that the Bible was sufficient for doctrinal guidance.*
  1. In January, 1519, he began a homiletical exposition of the New Testament in his sermons.
  2. Preaching from the Scriptures was an unheard of innovation in his day. This continued for four years.
  3. Zwingli's teaching was responsible for the Reformed Churches.
- C. *Difference in Luther and Zwingli.*
  1. Luther used the Bible as a corrective, retaining those rites and ceremonies of the Catholic Church which were not positively anti-scriptural.
  2. Zwingli used the Bible as a code of laws, rejecting everything not expressly enjoined in Scripture. His teaching included:
     a. Salvation by faith alone.
     b. Denial of the sacrificial quality of the mass and saintly intercession.
     c. Recognition of Christ as sole head of the church.
     d. Right of the clergy to marry.
     e. Abolishing images, relics, and organs from places of worship.
     f. The observance of the Lord's Supper as a symbolic or memorial supper.

II. **Work of John Calvin (1509-1564).**
- A. *Early life.*
  1. Born in Nayon, France, 25 miles NE of Paris. His father was an attorney.
  2. He first began the study of law but after two years, he changed to a study of religion.
  3. He was a devout student of the Bible and was influenced by the writ-

**Ulrich Zwingli (1484-1531)**

ings of Luther.
    4.   He became a leader among Paris Protestants but, because of opposition from the king, was forced to flee to Geneva, Switzerland.

B.  *Calvin soon rose to power in Geneva.*
    1.   He became a virtual dictator.
    2.   He endeavored to build Geneva into an ideal city through a system of "Christian Government."
    3.   A theological seminary was established in Geneva and from that institution young men went all over Europe preaching the doctrines of Calvin.

C.  *To people today, Calvin is best known for his "five tenets."*
    1.   Hereditary Total Depravity.
    2.   Predestination.
    3.   Limited Atonement.
    4.   Irresistibility of Grace.
    5.   Perseverance of the saints.

D.  *Calvin lives in history as a controversial figure.*
    1.   A contemporary once spoke of him: "Some think on Calvin heaven's own mantle fell, While others deemed him an instrument of hell."
    2.   Today, about the same attitudes are held toward what is known as "Calvinism." Some look on it as a blessing to man and some view it as one of the curses of religion.

E.  *Out of John Calvin's work, the Presbyterian Church was established.* A date is hard to give, but perhaps 1540 would be as good as any.

III.  **The Work of John Knox.**
A.  *Much of his early life is obscure.*
    1.   Born in Haddington, Scotland.
    2.   Ordained into the priesthood of the Roman Catholic Church.
    3.   Later embraced reformation principles and became one of the Royal Chaplains under Edward VI.
    4.   After "Bloody Mary" came to power, he fled to Germany and then to Geneva.
    5.   He became an ardent disciple of Calvin.

B.  *In 1559, Knox returned to Scotland.*
    1.   He carried Calvin's doctrines with him.
    2.   Established the Presbyterian Church in Scotland.

IV.  **Some Facts About the Presbyterian Church.**
A.  *There are nine divisions of Presbyterians in the United States.* There are three major bodies.
    1.   Largest is United Presbyterian Church in the U.S.A.
    2.   Presbyterian Church in the U.S. (Southern).
    3.   Cumberland Presbyterian Church.

B.  *Government.*
    1.   The Presbyterian Church received its name from its form of government. Each congregation has its own elders (*presbuteros* in Greek).
    2.   Authority, however, is in the Presbytery.
        a.   A certain number of churches belong to the Presbytery.
        b.   Each church has elders appointed to the board (Presbytery).
    3.   The highest judiciary of the church is the Annual General Assembly, made up of clerical and lay delegates elected by the Presbyteries.

C.  *Doctrines.*
    1.   Predestination (Quote from *Westminster Confession of Faith*, pp. 25-26): "By the decree of God, for the manifestation of his glory, some men and angels are predestinated unto everlasting life, and others fore-ordained to everlasting death. These angels and men, thus predestinated and foreordained, are particularly and unchangeably designed; and their number is so certain and definite that it cannot be

John Calvin (1509-1564)

either increased or diminished." (See Acts 10:34-35; Rom. 2:11; Rev. 22:17; Matt. 11:28-30; Jn. 3:16-17.)

2. Only the "elect" are saved (*Ibid.*, pp. 27-29). "Neither are any other redeemed by Christ, effectually called, justified, adopted, sanctified, and saved, but the elect only." (See 1 Jn. 2:2; Heb. 2:9; Tit. 2:11-12.)

3. Hereditary Total Depravity (*Ibid.*, pp. 41-43,72). "Our first parents, being seduced by the subtlety and temptation of Satan, sinned in eating the forbidden fruit. This their sins God was pleased, according to his wise and holy counsel, to permit, having purposed to order it to his glory. By this sin they fell from their original righteousness and communion with God, and so became dead in sin, and wholly defiled in all the faculties and parts of soul and body. They being the root of all mankind, the guilt of this sin was imputed, and the same death in sin and corrupted nature conveyed to all their posterity, descending from them by ordinary generation. From this original corruption, whereby we are utterly indisposed, disabled, and made opposite to all good, and wholly inclined to all evil, do proceed all actual transgressions." (See Matt. 18:3; 19:14; Ezek. 18:20.) "Man, by his fall into a state of sin, hath wholly lost all ability of will to any spiritual good accompanying salvation; so as a natural man, being altogether averse from that good, and dead in sin, is not able, by his own strength, to convert himself, or to prepare himself thereunto."

4. Direct operation of the Holy Spirit (*Ibid.*, pp. 45, 76). "Man, by his fall, having made himself incapable of life by that covenant, the Lord was pleased to make a second commonly called the covenant of grace; wherein he freely offered unto sinners life and salvation by Jesus Christ, requiring of them faith in him, that they may be saved, and promising to give unto all those that are ordained unto life, his Holy Spirit to make them willing and able to believe." "This effectual call is of God's free and special grace alone, not from anything at all foreseen in man, who is altogether passive therein, until, being quickened and renewed by the Holy Spirit, he is thereby enabled to answer this call, and to embrace the grace offered and conveyed in it." (A study of the New Testament will reveal that not a single person converted was enabled to obey by a direct operation of the Holy Spirit! The Spirit convicts and converts the sinner by means of the Word [Luke 8:11; 1 Pet. 1:22-25; Jas. 1:21; Eph. 6:17]. Note: that a person can resist the Spirit [Acts 7:51; 13:46; Lk. 8:11-15].)

5. Elect people can be saved without obedience (*Ibid.*, p. 77). "Elect infants, dying in infancy, are regenerated and saved by Christ through the Spirit, who worketh when, and where, and how he pleaseth. So also are all other elect persons, who are incapable of being outwardly called by the ministry of the word." (See Heb. 5:8-9; Matt. 7:21-27; 1 Pet. 4:17; 2 Thess. 1:7-9.) It is interesting to further note that they believe that the non-elect cannot be saved even though they are "called by the ministry of the word" (Ibid., p. 77). "Others, not elected, although they may be called by the ministry of the word, and may have some common operations of the Spirit, yet they never truly come to Christ, and therefore cannot be saved."

6. Perseverence of the saints (*Ibid.*, pp. 102-103). "They whom God hath accepted in his Beloved, effectually called and sanctified by his Spirit, can neither totally nor finally fall away from the state of grace: but shall certainly persevere therein to the end, and be eternally saved." (See 2 Pet. 2:20-22; Gal. 5:4; Heb. 6:4-6.)

7. Refer to the Lord's Day as the "Christian Sabbath" (*Ibid.*, pp. 130-131). "God hath particularly appointed one day in seven for a Sabbath, to be kept holy unto him: which, from the beginning of the world to the resurrection of Christ, was the last day of the week; and from the res-

urrection of Christ, was changed into the first day of the week which in Scripture is called the Lord's Day, and is to be continued to the end of the world as the Christian Sabbath."

    a. First day of the week at no time in the N.T. is referred to as "the Christian Sabbath"!

    b. No teaching anywhere that the Sabbath of the Old Testament was "changed into the first day of the week."

    c. The law that bound the Sabbath (Saturday) has been nailed to the cross (Col. 2:14-17).

    d. Christians must worship on the first day of the week (1 Cor. 16:1-2; Heb. 10:25; Acts 20:7).

8. Baptism (*Ibid.*, pp. 157-159). "Dipping of the person into the water is not necessary; but baptism is rightly administered by pouring or sprinkling water upon the person. Not only those that do actually profess faith in and obedience unto Christ, but also the infants of one or both believing parents are to be baptized. Although it be a great sin to contemn or neglect this ordinance, yet grace and salvation are not so inseparably annexed unto it as that no person can be regenerated or saved without it, or that all that are baptized are undoubtedly regenerated." (See Mk. 16:15-16; Acts 2:38; Col. 2:12; Rom. 6:3-4.) Thus they affirm three false doctrines: (1) that there are three baptisms: immersion, pouring, and sprinkling (Eph. 4:4); (2) that infants can be baptized; (3) that baptism is not necessary to salvation.

**Conclusion:**

1. Our study of church history ought to generate within us a greater appreciation for the church Jesus built.

2. These facts stand out in contrast to what we have seen develop:

    a. Jesus built the church; bought it with His blood (Matt. 16:18; Acts 20:28).

    b. Membership in the church of Christ is brought about by being saved (Acts 2:37-47).

    c. The organization, worship, and work of the church are all simple, and simply set forth in the pattern – the New Testament.

    d. Every member of the church is bound only by the Word of God (1 Cor. 4:6; 1 Pet. 4:11). Thus, the creeds of men have no power over Christians!

3. Why don't you obey Christ today?

## Questions

**Short Answer**

1. Explain the difference between Luther and Zwingli in regard to Bible authority. _____

_____

2. Some of Zwingli's teaching is included in this lesson. List the points with which you agree. _____

_____

_____

_____

3. Note the five tenets of Calvinism. With which of these five points do you agree?_____

_____

_____

_____

_____

4. According to Jesus in Matthew 7:24-29, why would some houses "stand" and

some "fall" when the storms come? _____
_____

5.  How would you prove that Jesus died for all sinners and not just the elect?
    _____
    _____

6.  Does a man become a drunkard (or whatever) because his father was such?
    _____

7.  Take any one of the conversions in the book of Acts and show how the Holy
    Spirit operated on the heart of the sinner._____
    _____
    _____

8.  The parable of the sower is found in Luke 8:4-15. Does this parable teach
    "once saved, always saved"? _____

9.  When a person is baptized, is there any power in water?_____
    If not, explain how "baptism saves" (1 Pet. 3:21): _____
    _____

10. Has the Sabbath been changed from Saturday to Sunday? _____

**Supply the Missing Word**
1.  Day on which to give and observe the Lord's Supper (1 Cor. 16:1-2; Acts
    20:7). _____
2.  Calvin's disciple. _____
3.  Passage that authorizes saints to assemble. _____
    _____
4.  Approximate date for origin of the Presbyterian Church. _____
5.  What the "seed" is according to 1 Peter 1:23? _____

**Matching**
_____ 1. Sabbath           A. Immersion
_____ 2. Baptism           B. Bought church (Acts 20:28)
_____ 3. Engrafted word    C. Lest ye fall (1 Cor. 10:12)
_____ 4. Take heed         D. Able to save (Jas. 1:21)
_____ 5. Blood             E. Saturday

## Lesson 10
# Baptist Church

**Introduction:**
I. In the last lesson we covered these points in Protestant history:
    A. Ulrich Zwingli responsible for the origin of the Reformed Church. The Congregational Christian Church and the Evangelical and Reformed Church have merged to form the United Church of Christ.
    B. Zwingli and Luther held opposing views regarding the authority of the Bible:
        1. Luther – anything acceptable that is not specifically forbidden.
        2. Zwingli – everything rejected that is not expressly enjoined.
    C. John Calvin and his disciple, John Knox, responsible for the origin of the Presbyterian Church in Switzerland and Scotland.
II. In this lesson we begin a study of the origin and doctrines of the larger religious bodies in this nation.

**Discussion:**
**I. The Origin of the Baptist Church.**
    A. *Baptist people are not agreed as to when the Baptist Church started.*
        1. Back about the beginning of the century, Baptists were generally agreed that the Baptist Church was started by John the Baptist in the wilderness of Judea. In 1902, a Baptist preacher by the name of J. N. Hall affirmed this position in a debate with A. G. Freed at Corinth, Mississippi.
        2. Most are now saying that it began during Christ's personal ministry.
            a. A Hazel, KY, Baptist wrote recently saying that Mark 3:13-14 is the beginning.
            b. H. Boyce Taylor, Sr., in *Why Be A Baptist* (p. 15) says: "John the Baptist prepared the material and the Lord Jesus organized the first Baptist Church during his personal ministry here upon earth."
            c. On page 17, Mr. Taylor says: "In Luke 6:12-16, after an all night of prayer, Jesus called His disciples unto Him and chose 12, whom He named apostles. They were called out from others. That is what *ekklesia* means, 'the called out.' They were chosen to be with Him (Mk. 3:14)."
                (1) Observe, however, that Mark 3:13-14 and Luke 6:12-16 are parallel passages to Matthew 10:1-15.
                (2) Some time *after* this, Jesus said, "I will build my church" (Matt. 16:18). In Matthew 16, the church had not yet been built!
        3. There are some Baptists who claim that there is an unbroken chain of Baptist Churches from the apostles till now (see *The Trail of Blood,* by J. M. Carroll).
    B. *Baptist scholars, however, readily admit that the Baptist Church cannot be traced back of the 17th century.*
        1. "The first regularly organized Baptist Church of which we possess any account is dated from 1607, and was formed in London by a Mr. Smyth, who had been a clergyman in the Church of England" (*Benedict's History of the Baptists*, p. 304).
        2. "The word 'Baptists' as a descriptive name of a body of Christians,

was first used in English literature, so far as is now known, in the year 1644. For the fact that the name Baptist comes into use at this time and in this way, but one satisfactory explanation has been proposed: it was at this time that English churches first held, practiced, and avowed those principles ever since associated with that name" (*Vedder's Short History of the Baptists*, p. 3).

3. "A history of Baptist Churches going further back than the early years of the 17th century would, therefore, in the present state of knowledge, be in the highest degree unscientific. The very attempt to write such a history now would be a confession of gross ignorance, either of the facts known, or of the methods of historical research and the principles of historical criticism, or both" (*Ibid.*, p. 5).

C. *John Smyth and Baptist beginnings.*
   1. Smyth was a member of, and a preacher in, the English Separatist movement.
   2. Persecution drove many Separatists to Holland, including Smyth and Thomas Helwys (1606).
   3. Among other things, Smyth believed in separation of church and state and rejected infant baptism.
   4. The Separatists had trouble and in 1608 Smyth, Helwys and about 36 others began a new group.
   5. "A refugee congregation of English dissenters settled in Amsterdam about 1607 and soon came under the influence of the Mennonites. From them they learned the biblical doctrine of believer's baptism. As a result, a Baptist congregation was established under the leadership of John Smyth and Thomas Helwys about 1608" (From a Baptist tract, *Who Are the Baptists?*, by Robert Torbet).
   6. In beginning this new group, Smyth "baptized" himself and the others by effusion (sprinkling).
   7. In 1611, Helwys returned to England and organized the first Baptist Church on English soil (A General Baptist Church).
      a. In 1633, the Particular Baptist (Calvinistic) Church was organized.
      b. In 1640, this English Church split and adopted immersion "as the mode of baptism."
      c. The name "Baptist" as a denominational title was first used in 1644 and was adopted then only by those who immersed.

D. *The Baptist Church in America.*
   1. Roger Williams came to America in 1631 as a Separatist minister. He contended for the separation of church and state.
   2. Persecution arose and he was banished from Massachusetts in 1636 and settled in Providence, RI.
   3. In 1639, a Particular Baptist Church was organized by Ezekiel Holliman, baptizing Williams and Williams baptizing Holliman and about a dozen others.
   4. At first Williams affirmed that they were nearer the "apostolic norm" than others, but later he became doubtful, withdrew, and remained a "seeker" the rest of his life.

E. *The Baptist Church has been beset by numerous divisions.* There are perhaps as many as 20 different groups in America.
   1. General, Particular, Christian Unity, Free Will, Primitive, Missionary.
   2. Independent, Seventh Day, Two Seed in the Spirit, Northern, Southern, etc.
   3. In view of the divisions among Baptists, all Baptists will not agree on the doctrinal points listed below.

## II. Baptist Doctrines.

A. *Original Sin* (infants are born depraved).
   1. "We believe that by the fall of Adam, all of his posterity are conceived in sin and brought forth in iniquity, so that every thought and every

imagination of the heart is only evil continually" (*Articles of Faith*, #3, First Baptist Church, Murray, KY).

2. Certain bodily ills may be inherited but our souls are affected by sin.
3. Our souls (spirits) are from God, not from our earthly parents (see Zech. 12:1; Eccl. 12:7; Heb. 12:9).
4. Man "inherits" the *penalty* for Adam's sin, not the *guilt*. All men die physically, must contend with weeds, and woman is subject to man and must bear children in sorrow (Gen. 3:16-19).

B. *Baptism.*
1. Baptism is not essential to salvation.
   a. "Baptism is not essential to salvation, for our churches utterly repudiate the dogma of 'baptismal regeneration'; but it is essential to obedience, since Christ has commanded it. It is also essential to a public confession of Christ before the world, and to membership in the church which is his body" (*The Standard Manual for Baptist Churches*, by Edward T. Hiscox, D.D., p. 20, Note 8).
   b. See Mark 16:15-16; Acts 2:37-41; 22:16; Rom. 6:3-4; Gal. 3:26-27; 1 Cor. 12:13; 1 Pet. 3:21.
   c. Note that baptism is essential to obedience but *not* essential to salvation. Therefore (by Baptist teaching) obedience is not essential to salvation (see Heb. 5:8-9; 1 Pet. 4:17; Matt. 7:21-27; 2 Thess. 1:7-9).
2. Baptism is essential to membership in the Baptist Church (see quote above).
   a. If baptism is essential to being in the Baptist Church but not essential to salvation, then being in the Baptist Church is not essential for salvation!
   b. Being in the church of the Lord is essential. In fact, being in the church and being saved are one and the same (Acts 2:47; 5:14; 20:28; Eph. 5:22-27).
3. Baptism must be administered by a Baptist preacher.
   a. "We believe that no person has a right to administer the ordinances (baptism and the Lord's Supper) but such as are regenerated, baptized, called of God to the work, and set apart by ordination, with the laying on of the hands of a presbytery" (*Articles of Faith*, #10, First Baptist Church, Murray, KY).
   b. Where does the New Testament give qualifications for the one doing the baptizing?
   c. Were Ananias (Acts 9:10-18), Philip (Acts 8:26-39), etc., Baptist preachers or gospel preachers?
4. Congregational approval by voting on all candidates for baptism.
   a. "It is most likely that in the Apostolic age when there was but 'one Lord, one faith, and one baptism,' and no differing denominations existed, the baptism of a convert by that very act constituted him a member of the church, and at once endowed him with all rights and privileges of full membership. In that sense, 'baptism was the door into the church.' Now it is different; and while the churches are desirous of receiving members, they are wary and cautious that they do not receive unworthy persons. The churches therefore have candidates come before them, make their statement, give their 'experience' and then their. reception is decided by a vote of the members. And while they cannot become members without baptism, yet it is the vote of the body which admits them to its fellowship on receiving baptism" (*Standard Manual for Baptist Churches*, by Edward T. Hiscox, D.D., p. 22).
   b. There is no command, necessary inference, or apostolic example for such a practice.
   c. See Acts 8:26-39. When the Eunuch asked to be baptized did

Philip say that such would have to wait until he could be voted on?

C. *Impossibility of Apostasy.*

1. "We believe that the saints shall persevere in grace, and never fall finally away" (*Articles of Faith*, #6, First Baptist Church, Murray, KY).

2. "Baptists believe that if a man is once saved he is always saved" (*Why Be a Baptist?* by H. Boyce Taylor, Sr., p. 13).

   a. This is another of Calvin's teachings. This doctrine came out of the Reformation and not the Bible.

   b. Read Heb. 3:12,19; 6:4-6; 10:26-31; Gal. 5:1-4; 1 Cor. 9:26-27; 10:12; 1 Tim. 1:18-20; 2 Tim. 2:17-18; 2 Pet. 2:1-3, 20-22; Gal. 5:19-21.

D. *Congregational Government of a Pastor and Deacons.*

1. "Baptists assert that the officers of a church are two, – and of right, can be no more, – pastor and deacons" (*Standard Manual for Baptist Churches,* by Edward T. Hiscox, D.D., p. 146).

2. In the church described in the New Testament, each local congregation had a plurality of elders and deacons (see Acts 14:23; 20:17; Tit. 1:5; Phil. 1:1).

3. The Greek word for "pastor" in the New Testament is *poimen* and is translated "pastor" and "shepherd" (see Eph. 4:11; 1 Pet. 2:25; 5:2).

4. In the New Testament church "pastors" and "elders" were the same!

E. *Conventions and Associations; Intercongregational and Intracongregational organizations; church Colleges and Hospitals; Missionary and Benevolent Societies.*

1. The New Testament knows nothing of anything smaller than, larger than, or other than the local congregation so far as a functioning unit is concerned.

2. Can you imagine Noah tying a half-dozen small boats on behind the ark – thus demonstrating his lack of confidence in the all-sufficiency of the ark God designed?

3. Read Acts 14:23; 1 Pet. 5:1-3; Acts 20:28; Eph. 4:12; 3:21; 1 Tim. 3:15; 1 Thess. 1:8; 2 Cor. 11:7-9; Phil. 1:5; 4:15-16; 1 Tim. 5:16; Acts 6:1-6; 11:27-30.

F. *Church sponsored Recreation, Entertainment, Meals, Church owned and operated Youth Camps* (see 1 Cor. 11:20-22, 33-34; Eph. 4:12; 1 Pet. 2:5).

G. *Youth churches, Choirs to sing to the Congregation, Instrumental Music in Worship* (see Acts 2:37-47; 5:14; Phil. 1:1; Heb. 2:12; Eph. 5:19; Col. 3:16).

H. *Lord's Supper.*

1. Close Communion.

   a. "Baptists believe in close communion. Jesus Himself was a close communionist. He did not invite His mother, or the man in whose house He instituted the Lord's Supper to be presented at that supper. How could you have closer communion than that?" (*Why Be A Baptist*, by H. Boyce Taylor, Sr., p. 13).

   b. Read 1 Cor. 11:20-30. "Let a man examine himself."

2. Frequency and time of observance.

   a. "As to the time, place, and frequency of the ordinances, no Scriptural directions are given. They are left optional with the churches. They are usually observed on Sundays, but not necessarily. As to the supper our churches have very generally come to observe it on the first Sunday of each month" (*The Standard Manual for Baptist Churches*, by Edward T. Hiscox, D.D., p. 20, note 5).

   b. Acts 20:7.

   c. This passage answers both questions:

      (1) When? "On the first day of the week."

      (2) How often? "On the first day of the week."

      (3) Each week has only one first day, but each week has one.

**Conclusion:**
1. In the days of the apostles, people were taught the gospel without addition or subtraction. When they obeyed it from the heart they became free from sin and were added to the church by the Lord (Rom. 6:17-18; Acts 22:16; 2:47; 18:8).
2. As obedient believers they were simply called Christians (Acts 11:26; 26:28; 1 Pet. 4:15-16).
3. They were never voted on and never joined any denomination.
4. They were just members of the family of God, which is the church (1 Tim. 3:15).
5. Our plea is that you come to Jesus in the same humble, obedient way today.

Notes

# Questions

**True or False**

_____ 1. The Baptist Church was started by John the Baptist.
_____ 2. When Jesus spoke the words of Matthew 16:18, the church had not yet been built.
_____ 3. A baby, when it is born, inherits the penalty for Adam's sin.
_____ 4. Baptism is essential to obedience but not to salvation.
_____ 5. Acts 8:26-39 is a record of the conversion of the Eunuch from Ethiopia.

**Underline**
1. John the Baptist's mission was (church-builder, fore-runner, saviour).
2. There are perhaps (30, 20, 10) different kinds of Baptist Churches in America.
3. (Hebrews 5:8-9, Luke 8:11, Ephesians 4:4-6) teaches that obedience is necessary to salvation.
4. The New Testament teaches that a child of God can fall from grace in (Colossians 3:1-2, Revelation 20:15, 2 Peter 2:20-22).
5. The Baptist Church is governed by (elders, deacons, saints).

**Short Answer**
1. About what date can be given for the origin of the Baptist Church? _____
2. Name some things a person may inherit from his parents. _____
   _____
3. What place does baptism hold in Baptist doctrine? _____
   _____
4. If a person can go to heaven without being a member of the Baptist Church, why does it exist? _____
   _____
5. Do Acts 20:28 (see verse 17) and 1 Peter 5:1-4 put elders or deacons over the local church? _____
6. In New Testament usage, does "pastor" identify an evangelist or an elder?
   _____
7. In Baptist doctrine, what is meant by "close communion"? _____
   _____
8. Would it be possible for Acts 20:7 to be the authority for only one Sunday assembly per month to observe the Lord's Supper? _____
   _____

*Baptist Church*                                                                    49

9. Did the Jews understand Exodus 20:8 to be authority to observe the Sabbath one time per month?. _____

10. Since there is no Bible authority for church-sponsored recreation, colleges, youth camps, etc., is it possible some churches of Christ have borrowed these things from the Baptists? _____

_____

## Lesson 11
# Methodist Church

**Introduction:**

I. Thus far we have studied in detail the origin of the following denominations:

A. Catholic Church, 606 A.D. – Rome, Italy.

B. Greek Orthodox Church, 1054 – Constantinople (Istanbul, Turkey).

C. Lutheran Church (First Protestant Denomination), 1521 – Whittenburg, Germany.

D. Church of England (Episcopal Church in America), 1534 – England.

E. Presbyterian Church, 1540 – Geneva, Switzerland.

F. Baptist Church, 1608 – Amsterdam, Holland.

II. As churches multiply, the religious confusion becomes greater.

A. Ephesians 4:4 states plainly that there is "one body" and that one body is the church (Eph. 1:22-23).

B. The church, the only church, the right church is the one revealed on the pages of the New Testament, and the one to which obedient believers are added by the Lord (Acts 2:36-47).

C. The only answer to religious confusion is back to the Bible. Study the Bible, believe the Bible, obey the Bible – pay no respect to the doctrines of men (Matt. 15:9) – and each one will be exactly what God intends.

III. In this lesson we study the origin of another major Protestant body – the Methodist Church.

**John Wesley (1703-1791)**

**Discussion:**

I. **Origin of the Methodist Church.**

A. *During the years 1719-1727, two brothers, John and Charles Wesley, were studying at Oxford University.*

1. They were the sons of a Church of England clergyman.

2. John was ordained a priest in the Church of England.

3. These young men, along with George Whitefield, began to meet together and formed a religious club.

4. They had no intention of starting a new denomination, but they were protesting the formality, coldness, indifference, and ungodliness in the Church of England.

B. *This group was given nicknames by other students: "Bible Moths," "Bible Bigots," and the "Holy Club."*

1. Because the members adopted strict methods of study, diet, exercise, etc., they were also dubbed "Methodists."

2. This is the name that eventually was chosen as their official name.

C. *Some historians give 1729 as the beginning. Others give 1737-1740.*

1. Historical Statement, *Methodist Discipline* (1908, p. 15): "In 1729, two young men in England, reading the Bible saw they could not be saved without holiness, followed after it, and incited others so to do. In 1737, they saw, likewise, that men are justified before they are sanctified; but still holiness was their object. God then thrust them out to raise a holy people. This was the rise of Methodism, as given in the words of its founders, John and Charles Wesley, of Oxford University, and

Presbyters of the Church of England."

2. "The Methodist Church is young, barely two hundred years old. It was born in 1738 when John Wesley's heart was strangely warmed at Aldersgate, in London, England" (from a Methodist tract, *The Methodist Church*, by James S. Chubb).

D. *In 1736, the Wesleys came to Georgia; Charles as a secretary to Gen. Oglethorpe and John as a missionary to the Indians.*

    1. This mission was largely unsuccessful, but on the ship John met a group of Moravians who inspired him by their piety.

    2. Upon returning to London two years later he attended a Moravian service in Aldersgate St., London. Here he heard Luther's preface to the book of Romans read.

    3. Wesley said, "I felt my heart strangely warmed; I felt that I did trust in Christ, in Christ alone for salvation; and an assurance was given me that He had taken away my sins, even mine and saved me from the law of sin and death."

    4. With this experience, Wesley was ready to propagate the doctrine of "faith only."

E. *As these men went out to preach, they found the pulpits of the Church of England closed to them.*

    1. They preached on the streets, in homes, barns, mining pits.

    2. Converts to their doctrine came thick and fast.

    3. In 1740, an old abandoned government building known as "the foundry" became the headquarters for the movement.

F. *Prior to the Revolutionary War, the Organization invaded the colonies.*

    1. Methodism "Americanized" quickly and grew during the war.

    2. Today the Methodist Church is divided into perhaps 15 to 20 groups, with a total membership exceeding 11,000,000 in the U.S.

## II. Organization.

A. *Local congregations called charges.*

    1. Trustees manage property interests; stewards handle finances and guide in spiritual affairs.

    2. The Pastor is appointed by the Bishop at the annual conference.

B. *Government invested in conference.*

    1. Quarterly – meets in local charge. Fixes salary of pastor; elects church officers; sets budget; sends delegates to annual conference.

    2. District – meets annually if authorized by the annual conference. Inquires into the spiritual condition, work, etc., of each charge.

    3. Annual – covers a defined geographical area. Ordains preachers; supervises pensions and relief. Every 4th year elects delegates to the General Conference.

    4. Jurisdictional – meets every four years. Main function, elect bishops.

    5. General – meets every four years. Law making body of the church.

## III. Doctrines.

A. *In 1784, the Methodist Church adopted its discipline.*

    1. It was an abridgement of the *Episcopalian Prayer Book*.

    2. In the 1908 edition (p. 3), this statement is made: "Dearly beloved brethren: it is our privilege and duty to recommend most earnestly this volume to you, which contains the *Doctrines and Discipline* of our Church, which we believe are agreeable to the Word of God, which is the only and the sufficient rule of faith and practice. Yet the Church, in the liberty given to it by the Lord, and taught by the experience of many years, and by the study of ancient and modern Churches, has from time to time modified its Discipline in order to secure the end for which it was founded."

    3. Then on page 4: "During the period in which this work has been extending, the Church has revised and enlarged its legislation to meet

the demands created by its own success."

4. Note: If the discipline and the New Testament taught the same, the discipline *could not* be modified (Deut. 4:2; Rev. 22:18-19; Gal. 1:8-9)!

5. An illustration of the changes in the Methodist Discipline:
   a. "Dearly beloved, forasmuch as all men are conceived and born in sin..." (M.D., 1908, p. 349).
   b. "Dearly beloved, forasmuch as all men are heirs of life eternal..." (M.D., 1948, p. 470). Note: Up until 1910, babies were born in sin and would go to hell if they died that way. Since 1910, they are born in Christ and will go to heaven. Babies began to be born differently in 1910, according to the Methodists.

B. *Baptism.*

1. Three "modes." "Let every adult person, and the parents of every child to be baptized, have the choice of either sprinkling, pouring, or immersion" (M.D., 1908, p. 349). (Read Col. 2:12; Rom. 6:4; see the meaning of the word "baptism" in the Greek.)

2. Infant baptism. "It (the Methodist Church) baptizes them (babies) in anticipation of their joining the church" (From *The Beliefs of a Methodist Christian*, by Clinton M. Cherry, p. 67).
   a. Not a single person was ever baptized in the New Testament who did not first believe, repent, and confess faith in Christ. (See every example of conversion in the book of Acts.)
   b. Actually, Methodists do not know why they baptize babies since they discarded Calvin's doctrine of inherited total depravity in 1910!
   c. Baptism is non-essential in Methodist doctrine. "No baptism is valid, regardless of its mode or the ritualistic words used, unless there is repentance, forgiveness, and a new life in God for the believer" (*Ibid.*, p. 68). (See Mk. 16:16; Acts 2:38; 22:16; Gal. 3:27; 1 Pet. 3:21.)

C. *Salvation by faith only.*

1. "Wherefore, that we are justified by faith only is a most wholesome doctrine, and very full of comfort" (M.D., 1908, Art. IX).

2. James says (2:24) that justification is "not by faith only." Which do you believe, James or the *Methodist Discipline*?

D. *Instrumental music.*

1. At the dedication of an organ in worship, the minister is to say, "In the name of the Father, and of the Son, and of the Holy Spirit, we dedicate this organ to the praise of Almighty God" (M.D., 1948, p. 550).

2. "In the name of" means "by the authority of." Where in the Word of God does the Father, Son, or Holy Spirit authorize the organ (or any kind of musical instrument) in the worship of the New Testament church?

3. The New Testament teaching concerning "music" is in the following verses: Matt. 26:30; Mk. 14:26; Acts 16:25; Rom. 15:9; 1 Cor. 14:15; Eph. 5:19; Col. 3:16; Heb. 2:12; Jas. 5:13.

E. *Jesus died to reconcile God to man.*

1. "Jesus truly suffered, was crucified, dead and buried, to reconcile his Father to us" (M.D., Art. II).

2. Read 2 Cor. 5:19-21. The Bible teaches that men are reconciled to God, not God to men. The Bible and man-made creeds always contradict each other.

F. *Members wear the name "Methodists."*

1. No such name authorized by Christ (see Acts 11:26; 26:28; 1 Pet. 4:16).

2. Any name but Christ's is inferior. There is salvation in no other name but Christ's (see Acts 4:11-12; Phil. 2:9-11).

## IV. Observe a Few of the Contrasts Between the Methodist Church and the Church of the New Testament:

| Methodist Church | Church of Christ |
|---|---|
| 1. Origin: England | 1. Origin: Jerusalem (Acts 2) |
| 2. Date: 1729 | 2. Date: 33 A.D. |
| 3. Founder: John Wesley | 3. Founder: Jesus Christ (Matt. 16:18) |
| 4. Name: Methodists | 4. Name: Christians (Acts 11:26) |
| 5. Baptism: Sprinkling and pouring | 5. Baptism: burial (Col. 2:12) |
| 6. Baptism: Infants and adults | 6. Baptism: believers who have repented (Mk. 16:16; Acts 2:38 |
| 7. Baptism: Non-essential | 7. Baptism: Necessary to be in Christ (Gal. 3:26-27) |
| 8. Authority: Methodist Discipline | 8. Authority: God's Word (1 Pet. 4:11) |
| 9. Salvation: Faith only | 9. Salvation: Obedience to the gospel (Mk. 16:15-16; Acts 2:38; Rom. 6:17-18; Heb. 5:8-9) |
| 10. Organization: One bishop ruling many churches | 10. Organization: Each church had plurality of bishops (Acts 14:23; 20:17; Tit. 1:5) |
| 11. Worship: Instrumental Music | 11. Worship: Singing (Eph. 5:19; Col 3:16). |

**Conclusion:**

1. As the Methodist Church is compared with Bible teaching, but one conclusion can be logically and faithfully reached – the Methodist Church is not the church the Lord established. Since there is only one way to heaven (Matt. 7:13-29), and since we only have one soul and only one opportunity to prepare here on earth for eternity, our prayer is that you will determine to study the Bible, obey its truths, and be nothing more than or less than the Word of God will make of you.

2. "Seek ye the Lord while he may be found, call ye upon him while he is near: let the wicked forsake his way, and the unrighteous man his thoughts and let him return unto the Lord, and he will have mercy upon him; and to our God, for he will abundantly pardon. For my thoughts are not your thoughts, neither are your ways my ways, saith the Lord. For as the heavens are higher than the earth, so are my ways higher than your ways and my thoughts than your thoughts" (Isa. 55:6-9).

# Questions

**Short Answer**

1. What two brothers were instrumental in beginning the Methodist Church?

_____

2. Give one example of the changes that have occurred in the *Methodist Discipline*. _____

_____

3. Were the churches in the New Testament period separate and independent, or were they tied together by some larger organizational structure? _____

_____

4. List the seven "ones" found in Ephesians 4:4-6. _____

_____

_____

5. State, in your own words, what Methodists believe about water baptism.

_____

_____

6. Does the Bible teach that we are justified by faith? _____
   Where? _____

7. How would you answer the argument that musical instruments were used
   in Old Testament worship and, therefore, can be used in the worship of the
   church? _____

   _____

8. According to 1 Peter 4:16, Acts 11:26 and 26:28, what name should the individual follower of Christ wear? _____

9. When Titus 1:5 and 1:7 are compared, what term means the same as "bishop"?_____

10. According to 1 Peter 5:1-4, to what is the oversight of an elder limited? ____

   _____

## Supply the Missing Word

1. To what is a person added upon his obedience to the gospel (Acts 2:47)?

   _____

2. The one passage in the New Testament where "faith" and "only" are used
   together. _____

3. The book that never needs changing or updating. _____

4. One pre-requisite to baptism that eliminates babies. _____

   _____

5. The one Jesus died to reconcile man to (2 Cor. 5:18-21). _____

## Multiple Choice

_____ 1. Methodist name: (a) God-given, (b) Nickname, (c) Chosen by Wesley.

_____ 2. Methodist congregation: (a) Charge, (b) Cell, (c) Lodge.

_____ 3. Methodist baptism: (a) Sprinkling, (b) Pouring, (c) Immersion, (d) All
         three.

_____ 4. Methodist music: (a) Vocal, (b) Vocal and instrumental, (c) Instrumental.

_____ 5. Methodist beginning: (a) A.D. 33, (b) A.D. 1901, (c) A.D. 1729.

## Lesson 12
# The Restoration

**Introduction:**

I. For several lessons we have studied the Protestant Reformation.
   A. When viewed from its stated purpose – to reform Romanism – it was a failure.
      1. Catholicism was too deeply entrenched to be reformed.
      2. After 450 years (from the days of Luther), Catholicism remains basically the same.
   B. However, the reformers accomplished good along with the evil.
      1. Evil came in the establishment of religious organizations unknown to the New Testament.
      2. Good came from the increased emphasis placed on Bible authority. The Roman Catholic Church was given a blow from which she has never recovered.

II. The close of the 18th and the beginning of the 19th centuries were marked by an intense spiritual fervor and a great revival of interest in religion. This was true both in America and in Europe.
   A. Good men were beginning to ask questions and to ponder the seriousness of religious division.
   B. A desire began to arise in many areas to "restore the ancient order of things."

III. The Restoration Movement was launched upon four basic principles.
   A. The acknowledgement of the New Testament Scriptures as the only authoritative rule of faith and practice. A positive attempt to obey the "pattern whereunto we have been delivered"; to accept only those things in religion which are *specifically prescribed* in the New Testament by command, apostolic example, or necessary inference.
   B. Renunciation of all human creeds and the acceptance of the precepts and examples of Jesus as the only creed binding upon Christians. Human creeds are by their very nature divisive; only the Scriptures furnish a rational basis for unity.
   C. The restoration of the apostolic or New Testament concept of the church in the minds of men. Worshipping and patterning our lives after the divine pattern.
   D. The union of all Christians upon the basis of the Bible.

IV. In this lesson we will notice the work of some of the men whose names are outstanding in the restoration period.

**Discussion:**

I. **James O'Kelly (1738-1826).**
   A. *O'Kelly was a Methodist preacher who worked in Virginia and North Carolina.*
      1. On many occasions O'Kelly found himself at odds with Francis Asbury, the Bishop.
         a. Asbury laid the rule of "pay, pray and obey" upon his laymen.
         b. O'Kelly wanted Methodist preachers to have the right to appeal to the Conference if they did not like their appointment.
      2. The Conference upheld Asbury and so O'Kelly, Rice Haggard, and

three other preachers withdrew from the Conference. This was in 1792.

    a. They formed a body known as the "Republican Methodist Church" (1793).

    b. In 1794 they held a meeting at Old Lebanon in Surry County, VA, at which they endeavored to devise a plan of church government. Finally Haggard stood up with a Bible in his hand and said, "Brethren, this is a sufficient rule of faith and practice. By it we are told that the disciples were called Christians, and I move that henceforth and forever the followers of Christ be known as Christians simply."

  3. Following Haggard's suggestion, a man by the name of Hafferty stood up and moved that they take the Bible itself as their only creed. From these two motions the O'Kelly movement devised what became known as the "Five Cardinal Principles of the Christian Church."

    a. The Lord Jesus Christ as the only head of the church.

    b. The name Christian to the exclusion of all party and sectarian names.

    c. The Holy Bible, or the Scriptures of the Old and New Testaments as the only creed, and a sufficient rule of faith and practice.

    d. Christian character, or vital piety, the only test of church fellowship and membership.

    e. The right of private judgment and the liberty of conscience, the privilege and duty of all.

B. *Weaknesses can be seen in these "Principles" but that these people were on their way back to the ancient order is evident.* The significance of O'Kelly and his work lies mainly in the direction he was looking.

## II. Elias Smith (Born in 1769 at Lyme, CT).

A. *Smith was a serious minded young man and in 1789 he became greatly concerned over the subject of baptism.* He was then baptized into the Baptist Church.

  1. Shortly thereafter, Smith began to preach for the Baptist Church. However, he had some misgivings about certain doctrines held by the Baptists.

  2. This motivated an intense investigation of Bible teaching. He then wrote: "When in my 24th year, I believed there would be a people bearing a name different from all the denominations then in this country; but what they would be called, I then could not tell. In the spring of 1802, having rejected the doctrine of Calvin and universalism, to search the scriptures to find the truth, I found the name which the followers of Christ ought to wear; which was Christians (Acts 11:26). My mind being fixed upon this as the right name, to the exclusion of all the popular names in the world, in the month of May, at a man's house in Epping, N.H., by the name of Lawrence, where I held a meeting and spoke upon the text, Acts 11:26, I ventured for the first time, softly to tell the people that the name, Christian was enough for the followers of Christ without addition of the words, Baptist, Methodist, etc."

B. *In October, 1802, the friends of Smith rented a hall in Portsmouth, NH, and began holding meetings there every Sunday.*

  1. On December 26, the hall burned down; they began to meet in a school house.

  2. They started with five members; by March they had grown to ten.

  3. Smith writes: "When our number was some short of twenty, we agreed to consider ourselves a church of Christ, owning him as our only Master, Lord, and lawgiver, and we agreed to consider ourselves Christians, without the addition of any unscriptural name."

C. *One of the amazing things about these activities was that the men involved had no contact with or knowledge of the others.* O'Kelly was unknown to Smith.

1. In 1803, Smith was visited by a medical doctor and Baptist preacher by the name of Abner Jones. Smith admitted that Jones' thinking had gone beyond his own in the matter of a return to New Testament authority.

2. In 1801, in Lyndon, Vermont, Jones had broken with the Baptists. He and others rejected human names and contended for the absolute authority of the New Testament.

3. After 1803, Smith and Jones joined forces in establishing churches free of denominational affiliation.

### III. Barton W. Stone (1772-1844).

A. *Stone was born at Port Tobacco Creek, MD.* His father died when he was three and the family moved to North Carolina.

1. When 18, he went to the famous school of David Caldwell near Greensboro in order to be admitted to the bar.

2. While there, he heard James McGready, a popular Presbyterian preacher, and a year or so later he joined the Presbyterian Church and began to preach.

3. Stone later moved to Cane Ridge, KY and was ordained.

   a. But even then, Stone had serious doubts about the scripturalness of the Confession of Faith – the creed of the Presbyterian Church.

   b. When asked at his ordination if he received the Confession of Faith, he replied, "I do, as far as I see it consistent with the Word of God."

B. *As Stone preached, he made his appeal directly to the Word of God.* He soon began urging the universality of the gospel and faith as a condition of salvation.

1. In 1801, plans were made for a great revival at Cane Ridge.

2. On Thursday and Friday before the third Lord's Day in August, the roads around Cane Ridge were crowded with wagons bringing people to the meeting.

3. It has been estimated that between 20,000 and 30,000 attended.

4. At this time, conversion had become almost a convulsion. The converts usually engaged in one of five "exercises."

   a. Falling exercise. The subject would cry out in a piercing scream and then fall flat on the ground and lay for several minutes as though dead.

   b. Jerking exercise. Various parts of the body would jerk violently to one side and then the other.

   c. Dancing exercise. This began with the jerks and then passed on to dancing. They usually danced until they fell exhausted to the ground.

   d. Barking exercise. The person's body jerked suddenly and violently causing a big grunt.

   e. Laughing and singing exercise.

5. As a result of the revival, trouble developed with the Presbyterian Synod.

C. *Stone and four others then withdrew from the Synod and formed a Presbytery of their own called the Springfield Presbytery.*

1. They drew up a document known as the "Apology of the Springfield Presbytery." In this they expressed their total abandonment of all authoritative creeds except the Bible.

2. Stone called his congregation together and informed them that he could no longer preach for them. He stated that he would continue to preach among them but not as a Presbyterian.

D. Within one year they began to see that they were wrong in forming another Presbytery.

1. On June 28, 1804, they issued the "Last Will and Testament of the

**Barton W. Stone (1722-1844)**

Springfield Presbytery."
2. This document contains less than 800 words but it is one of the most important to come out of the Restoration Movement.
3. This "Last Will and Testament" had 12 paragraphs. We quote five:
   a. "We will, that this body die, be dissolved, and sink into union with the Body of Christ at large; for there is but one Body, and one Spirit, even as we are called in one hope of our calling."
   b. "We will, that our name of distinction, with its Reverend title, be forgotten, that there be but one Lord over God's heritage, and His name one."
   c. "We will, that our power of making laws for the government of the church executing them by delegated authority, forever cease; that the people may have free course to the Bible, and adopt the law of the Spirit of life in Christ Jesus."
   d. "We will, that the people henceforth take the Bible as the only sure guide to heaven; and as many as are offended with other books, which stand in competition with it, may cast them into the fire if they choose; for it is better to enter into life having one book, than having many to be cast into hell."
   e. "We will, that all our sister bodies read their Bibles carefully that they may see their fate there determined, and prepare for death before it is too late."
E. *Stone and his group were looking toward New Testament Christianity but they were not allowed to make their journey in peace.*
   1. Evil reports were circulated about them.
   2. Nick-names were attached to them. For years they were referred to as "New Lights," a name widely used at that time to designate any off-brand religious sect.
   3. Stone also gave considerable attention to the subject of baptism and came to the conclusion that immersion was essential to salvation. For this conviction scorn was heaped upon him. On one occasion he wrote: "The floods of earth and hell are let loose against us, but me in particular. I am seriously threatened with imprisonment, and stripes I expect to receive for the testimony of Jesus, Kentucky is turning upside down." Again he said: "God knows I am not fond of controversy. A sense of duty has impelled me to advance it. In the simplicity of truth is all my delight. To cultivate the benevolent affections of the gospel shall employ my future life."

## IV. Thomas Campbell (1763-1854).
A. *Thomas Campbell was a preacher in the Seceder branch of the Presbyterian Church.*
   1. He was in poor health and came to America for relief.
   2. He arrived in Philadelphia in the spring of 1807. He presented himself to the Synod and was assigned to the Chartiers Presbytery in western Pennsylvania.
   3. He soon found himself preaching things contrary to Presbyterian doctrine. He opposed human creeds and contended for the all-sufficiency of the Bible.
   4. The Synod had several meetings to consider Campbell's heresy and finally on September 13, 1808, he was suspended from his ministerial office.
B. *Campbell continued to preach in homes of friends, school houses, in the open, etc.* In one of these meetings he closed his sermon with these words: "Where the Bible speaks, we speak, and where the Bible is silent, we are silent."
   1. When he sat down, there was silence. Then Andrew Munro spoke: "Mr. Campbell, if we adopt that as a basis, then there is an end to infant baptism." Campbell replied: "If infant baptism be not found in the

**Thomas Campbell (1763-1854)**

Alexander Campbell (1788-1866)

Scriptures, we can have nothing to do with it."

2. In 1809, this band of believers formed themselves into the "Christian Association of Washington." Campbell then wrote the *Declaration and Address* in which he set forth the famous slogan, "In faith, unity; in opinion, liberty; in all things, charity."

## V. Alexander Campbell (1788-1866).

A. *Alexander was born in Northern Ireland and was 20 years old when his father sent for the family to come to America.* They first tried to make the trip in 1808 but the ship was wrecked. They finally arrived in N.Y. in 1809.

1. Upon being reunited with his father, and having read the *Declaration and Address*, Alexander resolved to devote his life to studying the word and proclaiming it.

2. In 1810, the Brush Run meeting house was built and here he preached his first sermon.

B. *Soon the subject of baptism began to trouble Campbell.* He made an intense study of it and concluded that infants were not subjects of baptism, that the action was immersion, and that the confession the Eunuch made must precede it rather than the Baptist practice of telling an experience.

1. Campbell found a Baptist preacher, Matthias Luce, who was willing to baptize him.

2. When the day came, June 12, 1812, six others also asked to be baptized.

3. Soon practically the entire Brush Run church had followed suit.

C. *Being baptized made the Brush Run church both friends and enemies –* enemies among the Presbyterians and friends among the Baptists.

1. They were invited to join the Redstone Association of Baptist Churches. After much consideration they agreed to accept the invitations provided they be "allowed to teach and preach whatever they learned from the Holy Scriptures."

2. At first Campbell was held in high esteem by the Baptists and he defended their cause (immersion) against two Presbyterians in debate – John Walker and W. L. McCalla. In the Walker debate, Campbell introduced the idea that baptism is for the remission of sins and in the McCalla debate he pressed this truth in order to show that infants cannot be baptized since they have no sin. Shortly thereafter he declared that "baptism was never designed for, nor commanded to be administered to, a member of the church." This brought him into conflict with the Baptists.

3. The wedge between Campbell and the Baptists was also driven by his famous "Sermon on the Law."

a. Campbell was tried for heresy by the Redstone Association. He was acquitted, but wearied with strife, the Brush Run Church withdrew and joined the Mahoning Baptist Association in 1823.

b. By 1830, those who made up the Mahoning Association agreed on its unscripturalness and so they met and dissolved it.

c. When the break between Campbell and the Baptists came Campbell said: "We have always sought peace, but not peace at war with truth. We are under no necessity to crouch, to beg for favor, friendship or protection. Our progress is onward, upward, and resistless. With the fear of God before our eyes with the example of the renowned worthies of all ages to stimulate our exertions, with love to God and man working in our bosoms, and immortality in prospect, we have nothing to fear, and nothing to lose that is worth possessing."

d. Campbell was charged with starting another denomination. He wrote: "But a restoration of the ancient order of things is all that is contemplated by the wise disciples of the Lord, as it is agreed that this is all that is wanting to the perfection, happiness, and glory of the Christian community. To contribute to this is our most ardent desire – our daily inquiry and pursuit. Now in attempting this, it must be observed that it belongs to every individual and to every congregation of individuals to discard from their faith and their practice every thing that is not found written in the New Testament of the Lord and Saviour, and to believe and practice whatever is there enjoined. This done, and everything is done which ought to be done."

## VI. Growth and Uniting of Forces.

A. *We have dwelt with the problems and opposition that the restorers faced, but the other side of the picture is bright.*
   1. The truths that were being taught were readily grasped by the average person. People were anxious to discard the creeds of men, ready to abandon the churches of men, and be Christians and Christians only.
   2. People began to embrace New Testament Christianity by the thousands. Entire groups of denominational people were baptized for the remission of sins. One preacher reported 550 baptized in six months; another baptized 338 in six weeks; another assisted 222 to obey the gospel in 100 days. Walter Scott baptized 1,000 people in one year.
   3. The *N. Y. Baptist Register* of 1830 said that "one-half of the Baptist Churches in Ohio had embraced this sentiment." One Baptist preacher wrote to Campbell and said that he had traveled 2500 miles and had only found four Baptist preachers who had not been "corrupted."

B. *There were two mighty groups of people who pled for a return to the ancient order of things in the same part of the country.*
   1. Barton W. Stone and Alexander Campbell met for the first time in 1824. They discussed their differences and found them to be minor. They held each other in high esteem.
   2. In 1831, both groups met in Georgetown, KY, for one week. Raccoon John Smith, at this meeting, delivered one of the great speeches of his life. "God hath but one people on the earth. He has given to them but one Book, and therein exhorts and commands them to be one family. A union such as we plead for – a union of God's people on that one Book – must then, be practicable. Every Christian desires to stand in the whole will of God. The prayer of the Saviour, and the whole tenor of his teaching, clearly show that it is God's will that his children should be united. To the Christian, then such a union must be desirable. Therefore the only union practicable or desirable must be based on the word of God as the only rule of faith and practice.... For several years past I have stood pledged to meet the religious world, or any part of it, on the ancient gospel and order of things as presented in the Book. This is the foundation on which Christians once stood, and on it they can, and ought, to stand again. From this I can not depart to meet any man in the wide world. While, for the sake of peace and Christian union, I have long since waived the public maintenance of any speculation I may hold, yet not one gospel fact, commandment, or promise, will I surrender for the world. Let us then, brethren, be no longer Campbellites, or Stoneites, or New Lights, or Old Lights, or any other kind of lights, but let us all come to the Bible, and the Bible alone, as the only Book in the world that can give us all the light we need."

## Conclusion:
   1. All of this was done by *a group of men determined to sow nothing but the pure seed of the kingdom.*
   2. When pure seed is sown it is bound to reproduce after its own kind.
   3. The gospel of Jesus Christ is the seed of the kingdom (Lk. 8:11). When this seed was planted in the hearts of honest men and women in the New Testament period, it produced Christians. By the preaching of the word,

churches of Christ were established in every major city of the Roman Empire.

4. And so, by the preaching of the gospel, the church of the Lord was restored to the world.
5. May we realize that the hope of the world in this 20th century, is the same gospel. God help us to believe it, obey it, and then preach it to every creature under heaven.

## Questions

**True or False**

_____ 1. The Reformation was basically a success; the Restoration was a failure.

_____ 2. Human creeds were respected by men involved in the restoration effort.

_____ 3. The church revealed in the New Testament was the object of the restoration effort.

_____ 4. Such men as O'Kelly, Stone, etc., wanted to bring unity to a divided religious world.

_____ 5. Efforts toward restoration of the ancient order of things was achieved overnight.

**Underline**

1. Thomas and Alexander Campbell were (brothers, father and son, cousins)
2. The (New Testament, Old Testament, Gospels) is (are) the pattern for the church.
3. 1 Corinthians 1:10-13 is a plea for (growth, faithfulness, unity) among Christians.
4. The (Pope, Lord, Bishop) is the only head of the church.
5. The religious background of the Campbells was (Baptist, Methodist, Presbyterian).

**Short Answer**

1. In your own words, explain the difference between the Reformation and the Restoration._____
_____
_____

2. If a Civil War era house has fallen into disrepair, do you think it could be restored as it was originally if the blue prints still exist?_____

3. By using what "blue print" did the men mentioned in this lesson, hope to restore the church Jesus built? _____
_____

4. Name all the features of the New Testament church that needed restoring, that you can think of. _____
_____
_____

5. Would there by. any more Bible authority for calling oneself a Campbellite than a Lutheran?_____

6. We have heard it said that we are all going to heaven – just on different routes. Is this the teaching of Jesus in Matthew 7:13-14? _____
_____

7. In Genesis 1:11-12, we are told that seed produces after its own kind. According to Luke 8:11, what is the seed?_____

8. If the "seed" in the first century produced Christians (Acts 11:26), what will that

same "seed" produce today? _____

9.  In 1 Corinthians 14:33, we are told that "God is not the author of confusion, but of peace." Is God responsible for the division in the religious world today?

    _____

10. Study Mark 16:15-16, Acts 2:37-38 and 1 Peter 3:20-21. Is baptism for Christians or for those who are lost?_____

## Lesson 13
# Origin of the Christian Church

**Introduction:**

I.   In the last lesson we studied the efforts of men to "restore the ancient order."
   A.   James O'Kelly in Virginia and North Carolina.
   B.   Elias Smith and Abner Jones in the Northeast.
   C.   Barton W. Stone in Kentucky.
   D.   Thomas and Alexander Campbell in Pennsylvania, Virginia and West Virginia.

II.  In 1831, the mighty restoration forces of Stone and Campbell were united.
   A.   Previously, the two groups often met in the same town with little or no communion between them even though no basic differences separated them.
   B.   When people are sincerely dedicated to the proposition that the Bible alone will be the rule of faith and practice, division cannot long exist.

**Discussion:**

I.   **In the Restoration Movement, Two Different Ideas Regarding Cooperation Existed.**
   A.   *Stone, in 1804, had led in the dissolving of the Springfield Presbytery.* and had set his course toward a complete return to apostolic Christianity. He believed that churches could not be banded together in Associations, etc.
   B.   *Campbell, on the other hand, never lost his ardor for the theory involved in Baptist Associations.* When the Mahoning Baptist Association was dissolved in 1830, Campbell thought the action inconsiderate.
      1.   The *Millennial Harbinger* was published by Campbell beginning in 1830. Through its pages he had access to the brotherhood, and by this medium he kept laying before brethren his plan for "church cooperation."
      2.   In 1842, he wrote: "Now if Christ's kingdom consists of ten thousand families, or churches – particular, distinct, and independent communities – how are they to act in concert, maintain unity or interests, or cooperate in any system of conservation or enlargement, unless by consultation and systematic cooperation? I affirm it to be, in my humble opinion, and from years of observation and experience impossible."
      3.   Earl West, in his *Search For the Ancient Order* (Vol. 1, p. 159), says: "The church universal, as such, was not left with any specific work to do, but all work to be done was left up to local congregations. Hence, in New Testament times, the only organization of Christians to exist was a local church....Ecclesiasticisms unknown to the church owe their origin directly or indirectly to beginning with the church universal....For the brethren of a century ago to begin at this point and work toward general organizations was likewise to start on a false premise, and in these concepts the differences arose."
      4.   In 1843, Campbell presented his views on church organization by presenting a hypothetical case of a group of evangelists who go to an island called Guernsey. In five years they establish congregations A,

B, C, D, etc. After a while, Campbell says, these churches discover they cannot work efficiently without pooling their resources. A meeting is called at congregation A, and there the churches decided to band together and act in all matters just as one church.

5. It does not take an intelligent man to see that if the churches of one island could be banded together in order to act as one, then the churches of the world could be so banded together. Campbell, had he had it in his power, would have activated the church universal! There was one thing wrong with Campbell's plan – *he had no Scripture for it!*

C. As a result of Campbell's influence, Cooperation Meetings began to spring up all over the brotherhood. They were miniature missionary societies.

1. There was serious opposition to Campbell's ideas and to these "Co-operation Meetings." However, Campbell felt that he had the bulk of the brotherhood behind him, and early in 1849 he felt that the time had come to form a general organization for cooperation. He justified his position by beginning with the universal concept of the church and then saying that Christ gave no plan for the church, in this sense, to function; therefore the church is left free to devise its own plan.

2. In October, 1849, a Convention met in Cincinnati, Ohio, to consider the formation of a missionary society. Of the meeting W. K. Pendleton says: "We met, not for the purpose of enacting ecclesiastic laws, not to interfere with the true and scriptural independence of the churches, but to consult about the best ways for giving efficiency to our power, and to devise such methods of cooperation, in the great work of con-verting and sanctifying the world, as our combined counsels, under the guidance of Providence, might suggest and approve. There are some duties of the church which a single congregation cannot, by her unaided strength, discharge....A primary object being to devise some scheme for a more effectual proclamation of the gospel in destitute places, both at home and abroad, the Convention took under consid-eration the organization of a Missionary Society."

3. A. Campbell was elected the first president of the society.

D. *There was opposition from many quarters to this new body*, but perhaps the arguments were best summed up by Tolbert Fanning one of the found-ers of the *Gospel Advocate*. He said in that journal: "We believe and teach that the church of Christ is fully competent to most profitably employ all of our powers, physical, intellectual, and spiritual; that she is the only divinely authorized Missionary, Bible, Sunday School, Temperance and Coopera-tion Society on earth. It is, has been, and we suppose always will be our honest conviction, that the true and genuine service of God can be proper-ly performed only in and through the church. Hence, we have questioned the propriety of the brethren's efforts to work most successfully by means of state, district, and county organizations, 'Missionary,' 'Publication,' and 'Bible Societies' or Bible Unions, 'Temperance Societies, Free-Mason and Odd-Fellowship Societies' to 'visit' the fatherless and widows in their afflic-tion, and any other human organization for accomplishing the legitimate labor of the church."

II. **Disturbance Arose Among Brethren Over Instrumental Music in the Wor-ship.**

A. *Moves toward its use came slowly.* In 1851, a man who signed his name "W" wrote to J. B. Henshall, associate editor of the *Ecclesiastical Reform-er.* "Bro. Henshall – What say you of instrumental music in our churches? ...I think it is high time that we awaken to the importance of this subject. We are far in the rear of Protestants on the subject of church music. I hope, therefore, that you will give your views in extenso, on this much neglected subject."

1. Henshall replied: "In proportion as men become worldly minded, provided they have not entirely lost the fear of God, do they begin to

require helps to their devotion. That they would require such helps under a dark dispensation where they were rather lead into the use of symbolic rites, than inwardly illuminated by God's word and spirit, is not at all astonishing; but to say that we need them who live in the full light of the gospel privileges, and enjoy God's mercies and providence over us, is to say that we have no gratitude in our hearts and that we are every way unworthy of these benefits."

2. A. Campbell wrote in opposition to the instrument. In one essay he said: "I presume, to all spiritually-minded Christians such aids would be as a cow bell in a concert."

B. *To the church in Midway, KY, goes the "distinction" of being the first church to introduce it.* L. L. Pinkerton, the Midway preacher, said: "So far as is known to me. . . I am the only preacher in Kentucky of our brotherhood who has publicly advocated the propriety of employing instrumental music in some churches, and that the church of God in Midway is the only church that has yet made a decided effort to introduce it."

1. The singing was so bad at Midway that it would "scare even the rats from worship," Pinkerton said.

2. The congregation then began meeting on Saturday night to improve their singing and shortly afterwards someone brought in a melodeon to be in getting the right pitch. Before long one of the sisters accompanied the singing with her playing on the melodeon.

3. Then the group observed that the melodeon was good for the singing and so it was decided to use it on the Lord's Day.

C. *The advocates of instrumental music used two main arguments:*

1. The Old Testament authorized it. (The old law was nailed to the cross [Col. 2:14] and could no more be used to justify instrumental music than dancing, keeping the sabbath, animal sacrifices, temple worship, etc.)

2. It is expedient such as meeting houses and song books. (The error here lies in the fact that for a thing to be expedient, it must first be lawful! Song books are an expedient because singing is commanded. A meeting house is an expedient because an assembly is commanded. There is no command, approved apostolic example, or necessary inference for instrumental music; therefore the piano, melodeon, or organ cannot be an expedient. If there was authority to play in the New Testament, then the instrument would be an expedient!)

D. *As time went on, the opposition deepened.*

1. Moses E. Lard wrote in 1864: "What defense can be urged for the introduction into some of our congregations of instrumental music? The answer which thunders into my ear from every page of the New Testament is none. Did Christ ever appoint it? Did the apostles ever sanction it, or did any of the primitive churches ever use it? Never. In what light then must we view him who attempts to introduce it into the churches of Christ of the present day? I answer, as an insulter of the authority of Christ and as a defiant and impious innovator in the simplicity and purity of the ancient worship."

2. Lard also wrote: "But what shall be done with such churches? Of course, nothing. If they see fit to mortify the feelings of their brethren, to forsake the example of the primitive churches, to condemn the authority of Christ by resorting to will worship, to excite dissension, and give rise to general scandal, they must do it. As a body we can do nothing. Still we have three partial remedies left us to which we should at once resort: (1) Let every preacher in our ranks resolve at once that he will never, under any circumstances or on any account, enter a meeting house belonging to our brethren in which an organ stands. We beg and entreat our preaching brethren to adopt this as an unalterable rule of conduct. This and like evils must be checked,

and the very speediest way to effect it is the one here suggested. (2) Let no brother who takes a letter from one church ever unite with another using an organ. Rather let him live out of a church than go into such a den. (3) Let those brethren who oppose the introduction of an organ first remonstrate in gentle, kind, and decided terms. If their remonstrance is unheeded, and the organ is brought in, then let them at once, and without even the formality of asking for a letter, abandon the church so acting; and let all such members unite elsewhere. Thus these organ-grinding churches will in the lapse of time be broken down, or wholly apostatize, and the sooner they are in fragments, the better for the cause Christ."

III. **The Continued Progress of Liberalism and Complete Division.**
   A. *Any time brethren depart from divine authority in order to introduce one unauthorized practice, the door is left open for the introduction of others.*
      1. Earl West, in *Search For the Ancient Order* (Vol. 2), devotes 46 pages to the increase of liberalism.
      2. These things are mentioned:
         a. Fraternization with denominations.
         b. Denial of the verbal inspiration of the Scriptures.
         c. Teaching that the pious unbaptized would be saved.
         d. Sermons that did not sound a clear note. Sermons that took months of explaining as to what they meant and what they did not mean.
         e. The teaching that we are guided by the spirit of the New Testament – not by the letter. If you are sincere that is all that matters.
         f. Misconception of the nature of the church. The church, many came to believe, is just another sect and denomination as the rest.
         g. A drift toward a centralized ecclesiasticism that would serve as the "voice of the brotherhood."
   B. *The body of Christ was torn asunder.*
      1. The prayer of Christ (Jn. 17:20-21) was scorned.
      2. The entreaty of the Holy Spirit for unity was ignored (1 Cor. 1:10).
      3. The plea of the divinely inspired apostle was trampled under foot (Eph. 4:1-6).
      4. The United States government, in its census of Religious Bodies in America in 1906, recognized two separate bodies – the Disciples of Christ (Christian Church) and the church of Christ. Division was complete.
         a. The Christian Churches took their instruments and their missionary societies and walked a new course.
         b. As they did they took the bulk of the brotherhood with them.
         c. Brethren who contended for Bible authority in all matters were in the minority and most of the buildings were lost.
         d. The relatively few who still stood in the "old paths," "licked their wounds and looked to the future to start all over again."

**Conclusion:**
   1. May there always be men on this earth who, in kindness and with love in their hearts for the truth and the souls of men, will stand for the truth without fear.
   2. May God help us never to digress from the path of truth and righteousness.
   3. We urge those of you who have never come to Christ in obedience to His Word, to make this "the day of salvation."

# Questions

**Short Answer**

1. In Ephesians 4:4, we are told "there is one body." What is that one body according to Ephesians 1:22-23? _____

2. Do you think that, when men establish institutions (organizations) separate from the local church, and then tie them to the church, that Ephesians 4:4 has been violated?_____

3. Do you believe that the local church is capable of doing the things required by the Lord?_____

4. Does the church need a missionary society to aid it in preaching the gospel, a benevolent society to aid it in caring for its needy, or a college to aid it in edifying the saints?_____

5. After looking at Acts 11:26, 26:28 and 1 Peter 4:16, do you believe it is a scriptural use of the word "Christian" to describe a school, hospital, or a recreation center? _____

6. What were the two major issues that divided the Lord's church in the late 1800s? _____
_____

7. Can you find one New Testament passage that authorizes instrumental music in the worship of the church? _____

8. How would you answer the following arguments:
    a. Instrumental music can be used in the home. _____
    _____

    b. Instrumental music was used in Old Testament worship._____
    _____

    c. The New Testament does not say not to have it in the worship._____
    _____

    d. We should use any talent we have to praise God. _____
    _____

    e. The Psalms were accompanied by instrumental music._____

    f. Instrumental music aids the singing. _____
    _____

    g. Instrumental music is just an expedient._____
    _____

9. Generally, how do those who believe in human institutions and instrumental music identify themselves? _____

10. When this major division came, which group retained the largest membership and the most church buildings? _____
_____

**Multiple Choice**

_____ 1. In the first century, local churches were (a) Autonomous and independent, (b) Non-existent, (c) Tied together for efficiency.

_____ 2. The church universal has (a) responsibility to assemble for worship, (b) a specific work, (c) responsibility only as individuals.

_____ 3. (a) Stone, (b) Smith, (c) Campbell was elected president of the first missionary society.

_____ 4. In Proverbs 6:16-19, one of the things God hates is (a) Drunkenness (b) One that sows discord, (c) Fornication.

_____ 5. In 1 Corinthians 2:6-13, Paul teaches that the Scriptures are a (a) verbally, (b) partially, (c) naturally inspired book.

## Summarize Each Passage With One Word

1. John 17:20-21 _____
2. Colossians 3:16 _____
3. 2 Timothy 4:1-4 _____
4. 2 Timothy 2:15 _____
5. Romans 1:16_____

## Lesson 14
# Church History to the Present Day

**Introduction:**

I. In our last lesson we traced the division that came to the ranks of the Restoration Movement.
- A. Developed on two major points:
  1. Organization – missionary society formed.
  2. Worship – instrumental music added.
- B. Division recognized by our government in 1906.

II. We observed that, as time went on, the differences multiplied.
- A. Denial of verbal inspiration, miracles, etc.
- B. Open membership.
- C. Fraternization with denominations.
- D. Transition into just another denomination.

III. In this lesson, we look deeper into the causes of division and into present-day conditions.

**Discussion:**

I. **Basic Difference Between the Church and the Christian Church was Attitude Toward Authority.**
- A. *Historical background.*
  1. Martin Luther: "Whatever the Bible does not specifically forbid, we may practice."
  2. Ulrich Zwingli: "If the Bible does not authorize a practice, we must reject it."
- B. *When the Christian Church was formed, these two basic attitudes were the bases upon which "battle lines" were drawn.*
  1. Formation of the Missionary Society: Campbell and others reasoned as follows in regard to the organization of the church:
     - a. The church is referred to both universally and locally in the New Testament.
     - b. Local arrangement or organization is provided for in the New Testament.
     - c. Local churches acting independently can never accomplish their divine mission.
     - d. Therefore, there must be some means devised in order that local churches may act together.
     - e. Since no revelation has been given to tell us how, we are free to devise a plan. In other words, the Bible does not tell us how to organize the church universal, so we may do it as we please!
  2. In regard to the introduction of the instrument into the worship, many of the arguments in favor could be summed up with: "The Bible does not tell us not to have it."
- C. *One is reminded today of our brethren who write tracts and articles entitled "Where there is no pattern."* If there is no pattern, there is no authority, and if there is no authority, man cannot move.
  1. Scripture limits a person to what is written:
     - a. 1 Corinthians 4:6.
     - b. Ephesians 3:1-4.

     c.   John 20:30-31.
     d.   1 Timothy 3:16-17.
     e.   2 John 9.
  2.   Man cannot add to or subtract from the word of God (Deut. 4:2; Rev. 22:18-19).

II. **Our Present-day Difficulties in the Church Find Their Origin in the Same Historic Difference in Attitude Toward Authority.**
  A.  *Organization.*
    1.   Institutionalism. Today we find the church establishing and maintaining organizations of various kinds:
      a.   Benevolent institutions:
        (1)  Old Folks Homes.
        (2)  Widows Homes.
        (3)  Orphans Homes, etc.
      b.   Social service institutions:
        (1)  Hospitals.
        (2)  Homes for unwed mothers, etc.
      c.   Educational institutions:
        (1)  Kindergartens.
        (2)  Grade schools and high schools.
        (3)  Colleges.
        (4)  Schools of preaching, etc.
    2.   Sponsoring church arrangements:
      a.   Example:
        (1)  "Herald of Truth" sponsored by Highland Avenue church in Abilene, Texas.
        (2)  Area-wide evangelistic efforts. Each one has a sponsoring church.
      b.   Here are some of the reasons why such are wrong:
        (1)  Such an arrangement constitutes a violation of the autonomy, equality, and independence of local churches.
        (2)  Such an arrangement ignores the limitations placed on elders (Acts 20:28; 1 Pet. 5:1-4).
        (3)  There is no more authority for activating the church universal through one eldership or one local church, than through the Missionary Society.
        (4)  Such "cooperation" has no scriptural authority (Acts 11:22-23, 27-30; Rom. 15:25-32; 1 Cor. 16:1-2; 2 Cor. 8-9; 11:8).
  B.  *Work.*
    1.   Churches across the land are involving the church in recreation entertainment, and all sorts of social activities.
      a.   Summer camps.
      b.   Student centers located near colleges and universities.
      c.   Youth rallies.
      d.   Bowling, baseball teams, etc. Some churches employ a "recreation director."
    2.   Hundreds of churches provide facilities (and often the food) to feed "rich" people (see 1 Tim. 5:16).
    3.   Interesting to walk the parking lot of Opry Land and see the number of "Church of Christ Buses" that have (at church expense) hauled kids.
    4.   Common today for preachers to plead with churches to "minister to the whole man."
    5.   Notice the parallel between the work and worship of the church.

| Worship | Work |
|---|---|
| Sing – Eph. 5:19<br>Pray – Acts 2:42<br>Teach – Acts 20:7<br>Give – 1 Cor. 16:1-2<br>Lord's Supper – Acts 20:7 | Preaching – 1 Tim. 3:15<br>Edification – Eph. 4:16<br>Benevolence – Acts 4:32-37<br>Discipline – 1 Cor. 5 |

*To these nothing can be added or subtracted.* You can no more add recreation to the work, than you can instrumental music to the worship.

**Conclusion:**
1. The seed that produced the Christian Church has been planted again.
2. Luther and Zwingli could not agree 450 years ago. These basic attitudes toward authority continue to divide people in this generation.
3. Here is where authority directs:
   a. There is one body (Eph. 4:4). That one body has been so arranged or organized that it can function according to God's plan.
   b. That one body has been given responsibilities in the areas of worship and work.
4. What is your attitude toward the authority of Christ? Must we speak where the Bible speaks and be silent when it is silent?
5. Do we walk by faith or by sight?

## Questions

**True or False**
1. The basic difference between the church of Christ and the Christian Church is instrumental music.
2. Attitude toward authority is only a minor consideration in the division that exists.
3. Religiously, man is not allowed to go beyond what is written (1 Cor. 4:6).
4. The local church should make arrangements for unwed mothers.
5. Recreation and entertainment are home responsibilities.

**Supply Missing Word or Words**
1. What Revelation 22:18-19 forbids. _____
2. Responsible for secular education. _____
3. Not to be charged in 1 Timothy 5:16. _____
4. The recipients of church benevolence in Romans 15:26. _____
5. Numbers of acts of public worship. _____

**Short Answer**
1. In Revelation 2, 3, letters to seven churches are found. How many of these received no rebuke? _____
2. In Revelation 2:5, what is meant by "will remove the candlestick out of its place"? _____
3. If a local church is to remain a church of Christ, what must it do? _____
4. Years ago it was common to hear the statement made that "the Christian Church had a piano leg in the door and couldn't close it." What was meant by that? _____

5.  What is meant by the phrase "social gospel"? _____
    _____
    _____

6.  Can you give an example of scriptural church cooperation and one of unscriptural church cooperation? _____
    _____
    _____
    _____

7.  Would you say that any scheme that would endeavor to activate the church universal is unscriptural? _____
    _____

8.  Which is worse – to corrupt the worship of the church or the work of the church? _____

9.  Each local church is composed of members and is responsible for worship, work, financial resources, and discipline. Which of these can be transferred to the oversight of elders in another local church? _____

10. Do you believe that the slogan, "We speak where the Bible speaks, and are silent where the Bible is silent," is a scriptural concept?_____
    _____